SOUTH-EAST ASIAN SOUPS

SOUTH-EAST ASIAN SOUPS

THAILAND, MALAYSIA, SINGAPORE INDONESIA, VIETNAM, CAMBODIA

TERRY TAN

LORENZ BOOKS

This edition is published by Lorenz Books,
an imprint of Anness Publishing Ltd,
108 Great Russell Street, London WC1B 3NA;
info@anness.com

www.lorenzbooks.com; www.annesspublishing.com;
twitter: @Anness_Books

If you like the images in this book and would
like to investigate using them for publishing,
promotions or advertising, please visit our website
www.practicalpictures.com for more information.

© Anness Publishing Ltd 2016

A CIP catalogue record for this book
is available from the British Library.

Publisher: Joanna Lorenz
Senior Editor: Felicity Forster
Recipes: Ghillie Başan, Judy Bastyra, Becky Johnson, Vilma Laus
   and Terry Tan
Photographers: Martin Brigdale, Nicki Dowey and William Lingwood
Designer: Nigel Partridge
Production Controller: Pirong Wang

PUBLISHER'S NOTE
Although the advice and information in this book are believed
to be accurate and true at the time of going to press, neither the
authors nor the publisher can accept any legal responsibility or
liability for any errors or omissions that may have been made nor
for any inaccuracies nor for any loss, harm or injury that comes
about from following instructions or advice in this book.

COOK'S NOTES

Bracketed terms are intended for American readers.

For all recipes, quantities are given in both metric and
imperial measures and, where appropriate, in standard
cups and spoons. Follow one set of measures, but not
a mixture, because they are not interchangeable.

Standard spoon and cup measures are level.
1 tsp = 5ml, 1 tbsp = 15ml, 1 cup = 250ml/8fl oz.

Australian standard tablespoons are 20ml. Australian
readers should use 3 tsp in place of 1 tbsp for
measuring small quantities.

American pints are 16fl oz/2 cups. American readers
should use 20fl oz/2.5 cups in place of 1 pint when
measuring liquids.

The nutritional analysis given for each recipe is
calculated per portion (i.e. serving or item), unless
otherwise stated. If the recipe gives a range, such as
Serves 4–6, then the nutritional analysis will be for
the smaller portion size, i.e. 6 servings. The analysis
does not include optional ingredients, such as salt
added to taste.

Medium (US large) eggs are used unless
otherwise stated.

Front cover shows Spicy Tripe Soup with Lemon Grass
and Lime – for recipe, see pages 64–5.

CONTENTS

Introduction	6	Thailand	24
Vegetables and fruits	10	Malaysia	38
Poultry and meat	12	Singapore	46
Fish and shellfish	14	Indonesia	54
Tofu	16	The Philippines	66
Rice	17	Vietnam	74
Noodles and wrappers	18	Cambodia	88
Herbs and spices	20		
Flavourings and sauces	22	Index	96

Introduction

Ascribing South-east Asian soup to the genre of 'liquid sustenance' falls far short of its importance. The basis of most soups from this region lies in two omnipotent products grown throughout South-east Asia – coconut and tamarind. Underscoring most soups, coconut gives milk extracted from its white meat, and tamarind imparts its fragrant tartness when mixed with water. Despite their important roles as base stocks, these are but blank canvases without the plethora of herbs and spices that sizzle up soups.

Four plates and a bowl

Within the pantheon of Chinese culinary practices, herbal soups have always been cherished for their restorative medicinal powers. But even without the inclusion of curative elements, the regard for soups pays homage to TCM or Traditional Chinese Medicine, which is based on the tenet of Yin-Yang. This is a philosophy that promulgates a universal balance of the body politic. It dictates that every dish should be the balanced sum of opposites. Thus, dry needs to be tempered with wet; sweet with sour; and crunchy with soft; and so on. When one imbibes soup, Yin-Yang is established, and all is well.

There is an old saying among the Chinese that perhaps explains this reverence more succinctly. When referring to a meal, the almost poetic description of 'four plates and a bowl' places soup at the very centre of table culture. Each soup may have started in some rustic kitchen as no more than simple sustenance. Drunk throughout a meal rather than as a starter, its key

role is to 'refresh the palate for what is to come'. Through trial and error, ever more intriguing flavours began emerging. Home cooks and chefs became more inspired to try new recipe ideas. Meanwhile, Hindu Ayurvedic principles were fathoming the efficacy of many spices to a profound degree. In tandem with Yin-Yang philosophy, these two original culinary schools have enriched the South-east Asian pot no end.

The soup trail

At the beginning of this soup journey around South-east Asia, tribute must firstly be paid to the two ancient civilizations of India and China, which provided their core gastronomies to South-east Asian tables today. These Indo-Chinese beginnings were the true touchstones of the progeny cuisines. Down the centuries, food became much more than basic sustenance. Many generic dishes spawned hybrids with

Above *South-east Asian soups often begin with tamarind stock. When combined with ingredients such as shellfish, chilli, turmeric and lemon grass stalks, a quintessential spicy flavour results.*

an inevitable potpourri of flavours and textures. They were adapted, tweaked, perfumed and spiced up to become the cornucopia of flavours across the region.

Not for nothing are the Molucca Islands within Indonesia called the Spice Islands. Spices such as nutmeg, mace and cloves were found only here. With the opening of the Silk and Spice Routes that pre-dated Christianity, cassia, cardamom, ginger, cloves and cinnamon became desirable merchandise. These sprawling islands were and still are the fount of spices for global tables.

More than any other ingredient, the coconut has reigned supreme in Asian kitchens for centuries. Its sobriquet

Above *Spices such as lemon grass and chilli give many South-east Asian soups their distinctive flavour and colour.*

'The Tree of Life' is truly earned. The leaves are used as wrappers for all manner of foods and as thatching, their spines become skewers for meat, the nut yields milk, sap from its flowers are churned into palm sugar, and even uprooted trunks provide building material.

Fundamentally, cuisines evolved on the backs of indigenous produce. As people became more mobile and settled here, there and beyond, they may have taken with them only their clothes on their backs, but also their treasured recipes. From expediency came the creation of ever more recipe ideas, stemming from the culinary founts. Merchants from India and the Middle East had been trading along coastal South-east Asia in areas which already featured some inter-racial communities and their resulting cuisines. This trading dates as far back as the 6th century, when the Hindu Sri Vijaya kingdom ruled most of the region from their seat in Sumatra. Hindu Buddhism was established throughout Indo-China.

Wild or farmed throughout South-east Asia, the fecundity of indigenous produce such as rice, lemon grass, chillies, galangal, shallots and an intoxicating range of aromatics infused each family pot with wonderful bouquets. This plethora of flavours and textures enhanced both traditional and emerging cuisines, creating hybrid gems that people around the world enjoy today.

Throughout the Indonesian Archipelago and as far-flung as East Timor, cuisines are fairly similar and rest largely on spice blends. Even on Christmas Island, where the population of several thousand people is mostly of Chinese and Malay stock, food is reflective of either Chinese or a Malaysian culinary elements.

The big picture is certainly one to salivate over. It is no idle boast that the range of South-east Asian dishes is vast compared to that of Western gastronomies. One can tweak a Chinese, Thai or Malaysian dish at will to produce amazing and new tongue-tingling results. The same cannot be said of a steak dinner bereft of anything but salt and pepper.

Evolution has put a resounding stamp on countless dishes and soups: Thai rice porridge that once hailed from North China; fish ball soup that had its beginnings in China's eastern province; iconic Singapore laksa that is a luscious amalgam of Indian influences, Thai elements and Indonesian curries harking back to earlier Indian kitchens; Filipino snacks that are intriguingly of Malay, Spanish and American nuances; and Vietnamese and Cambodian soups and broths that are alchemies of pots from neighbouring Myanmar, Laos and Thailand.

Below *This Malaysian market is bustling with shoppers buying all manner of fresh vegetables, herbs and spices.*

Thailand

Soups from Thailand are at once savoury, hot and spicy, as cooks are adept at marrying different flavours together. Be it rice, noodles or root vegetables, the combination of different textures and seasonings is the hallmark of the cuisine. Herbal keynotes come from lemon grass, galangal, peppery basil and the ever-present chillies. Kaffir lime leaves are liberally used for their distinctive lemony scent. Fish sauce is a salting agent that Thais are inordinately fond of. Called *nam pla* in Thai, it is similar to the *nuoc cham* of Vietnam.

Malaysia

This region is divided into two main parts: Peninsula Malaysia and the contiguous states of Sabah and Sarawak, which occupy most of the northern coast of the island of Borneo, which in turn also cradles Brunei, an independent sovereign state. The cooking throughout the region is basically similar. Malaysian

Below *A laksa consists of noodles in a coconut broth; this one also has seafood.*

Above *This Malaysian soup contains seafood, pork and won ton wrappers.*

soups are reminiscent of Indonesian and Thai dishes employing much the same blends, but with prominent seafood flavours. Won ton soup is Chinese in essence, and can be found all over Malaysia and Singapore as a favourite snack. With reference to the Yin-Yang philosophy, imbibing the root vegetable mooli promises to dispel excess body heat. As more new settlers spread

across South-east Asia, their cooking incorporated indigenous products, and many hybrids were born that also crossed regional borders. Today you are likely to find dishes common to several countries.

Singapore

As a thriving hub of South-east Asia, Singapore has earned the reputation of being a gourmet paradise. Many favourite dishes here hailed from China and Indonesia, and some are tempered with colonial nuances. Eurasian curried soup reflects colonial history – the inter-racial community of people born of European, Indian, Chinese and Malay bloodlines. An all-time favourite is Hokkien prawn noodle soup, which originated in the Fujian province of South China. The term 'Hokkien' is simply the dialectic pronunciation of the Mandarin 'Fujian'. Of all the soups here, one must count as truly iconic: laksa is an Indonesian- and Thai-inspired noodle dish redolent with a complex spice blend of onions, garlic, chillies and turmeric simmered in coconut milk with galangal, lemon grass and pungent shrimp paste. This paste, known as *kapi* (Thai) or *belacan* (Malay), is widely used in Thai, Malaysian and Indonesian cooking.

Indonesia

Across the Indonesian Archipelago and including East Timor and Christmas Island, spices come into their own. Local fruits such as papaya or pawpaw, tapioca and corn are artfully cooked with coconut milk, tamarind water, lime juice, galangal, turmeric, cloves, pepper and many fresh herbs. When travelling through the region, one is apt to come upon itinerant food vendors in rural areas and food centres in urban areas selling these dishes.

The Philippines

Although a little distant geographically, soups from the Philippines echo much the same herbal top notes. Filipinos are enamoured of sour flavours, and their sinigang soup is practically a national dish. The thousands of islands that make up the country are blessed with a tropical climate where much the same produce is grown as in the whole of South-east Asia. Rice is the basic staple, and seafood plays a large part in soupy recipes. Poultry, beef, pork, leafy and root vegetables and papayas are all given fragrant touches of chillies, vinegar, tamarind and ginger.

Vietnam

A favourite Vietnamese breakfast staple is soup – not merely a palate teaser, but enjoyed as a round-the-clock snack. The cuisine is largely Chinese in origin, but it also speaks eloquently of Laotian, Thai and Cambodian nuances. While winter melon soup features lily buds – a traditional Chinese ingredient – the fragrance comes from coriander (cilantro) and mint. Some soups are

Below *This Filipino sinigang is made with tamarind paste, pork and vegetables.*

so substantial they are practically stews, as in roast duck broth with noodles. This is truly a marriage of ideas, in which Cantonese roast duck is soused with ginger, chillies, fish sauce, lemon grass and fillip, a garnish of marinated chillies.

Cambodia

Also known as Khmer cuisine, Cambodian cooking is probably less known than that of her neighbouring countries, because the country was torn by strife for decades and suffered long spells of isolation. Nonetheless, her cuisine is delightful and intoxicating, with flavours straddling Chinese and Thai kitchens. There are rustic notes to the cooking employing freshwater fish, bamboo shoots, rice, galangal and lemon grass. These last two ingredients are fundamental to Cambodian flavours. Duck and preserved lime soup is a typical case in point about hybrid and cross-border cooking. The same soup is a Singapore and Malaysian favourite, and is believed to originate in the Chiu Chow region of South China. The Chiu Chow or Teochew people are known for their soups.

Below *Lily buds are combined with winter melon in this Vietnamese soup.*

Above *Cambodian duck and preserved lime soup originally came from China.*

Myanmar and Laos

Like Cambodia, both Myanmar and Laos have, unfortunately, suffered much turmoil, resulting in less mobility of their cuisines. Myanmar menus are culled from both Indian and Chinese genres, with prominent use of chickpea flour as a thickener. Generally, Myanmar soups are much less spicy due to the subtle use of turmeric and ginger rather than chillies. Laotian cuisine takes a large leaf from her Thai neighbour, particularly the north-east region of Isaan. Here, there is much use of esoteric ingredients such as pickled bamboo shoots and banana palm hearts. The cuisine is marked by sharp, hot and bitter flavours.

In this book

Be it rustic hawker fare or sophisticated restaurant star dish, humble or imperial; whether thin and light or chunky and robust, there's much to be enjoyed in the pages that follow. There is free licence to tweak each soup to suit your tastes, much as the recipes have undergone the same process themselves over the centuries.

Vegetables and fruits

South-east Asian cooks use vegetables freely in soups; there is an abundant choice of varieties in both markets and supermarkets. Some recipes also include fruits – the hot, sweet and sour soups of Vietnam and Cambodia, for example.

Chinese leaves

Also known as Chinese cabbage or Napa cabbage, these have pale green, crinkly leaves with long, wide, white ribs. They are pleasantly crunchy and have a sweet, nutty flavour. Look out for firm, slightly heavy heads with pale green leaves without blemishes or bruises.

Pak choi

There are several varieties of pak choi, also known as bok choi. Unlike Chinese leaves, it doesn't keep well, so use it within a day or two. The vegetable is generally cooked, although very young and tender pak choi can be eaten raw.

Below *When cooked, Chinese leaves lose their subtle taste and take on the flavour of the other ingredients in the soup.*

Above *Pak choi is known by many names, including bok choi, horse's ear, Chinese cabbage and Chinese white cabbage.*

Above *Choi sum is often sold in bunches. Its leaves can be sliced, but more often they are steamed whole.*

Choi sum

A brassica with bright green leaves and thin, pale, slightly grooved stems, choi sum has a pleasant aroma and mild taste, and remains crisp and tender if properly cooked.

Chinese broccoli

With its somewhat straggly appearance, this brassica looks more like purple sprouting broccoli than prim Calabrese. It goes by the common Cantonese name of *kai lan*, and every part of the vegetable is edible.

Aubergines

Popular throughout South-east Asia, aubergines (eggplants) come in a variety of shapes, sizes and colours, especially in Thailand where they range from pea-sized to 30cm/1ft long green and purple-streaked types. They have a smoky, slightly bitter taste, and spongy flesh that absorbs other flavours and oils.

Mooli

Also known as daikon, this Asian vegetable looks rather like a parsnip, but is actually related to the radish. The flavour is milder than that of most radishes, however, although the texture is similar: crisp and crunchy.

Bamboo shoots

Fresh bamboo shoots are quite hard to buy outside Asia, but you may find them in big-city Asian markets. They must be parboiled before being cooked, as the raw vegetable contains a highly toxic oil. Canned bamboo shoots are easily available in all Asian supermarkets and need only be drained before use.

Water chestnuts

Fresh, crisp water chestnuts are the corms of a plant that grows on the margins of rivers and lakes. Their snow-white flesh stays crunchy even after long cooking. Fresh water chestnuts

Above *Mooli is used in Malaysian soups to dispel body heat.*

are often available from Asian markets. They keep well in a paper bag in the refrigerator. Once released from their dark brown jackets, they must be kept submerged in water in a covered container and used within one week. Canned water chestnuts should be rinsed before being used.

Beansprouts

Sprouted from mung beans, beansprouts are often combined with noodles throughout South-east Asia. Soy bean sprouts are less common and have larger heads. They should be used within two days. Better still, sprout the beans yourself by soaking dry mung beans in a little water for a week or so. Before use, rinse them to remove the husks and tiny roots.

Spring onions

Slender and crisp, spring onions (scallions) are appreciated by Asian cooks not only for their aroma and flavour, but also for their perceived cooling qualities.

Right *Shiitake mushrooms are used in many Vietnamese soups, often in combination with tofu, to add substance and flavour to the dish.*

Mushrooms

Several types of mushrooms are used in South-east Asian soups, and many of these are now widely available. Shiitake mushrooms are prized in Asia, both for their flavour and their medicinal qualities. They have a slightly acidic taste and a meaty, slippery texture. They contain twice as much protein as button (white) mushrooms, and their robust flavour makes them the ideal partner for noodles and rice. Oyster mushrooms have a mild flavour and are pastel-coloured in shades of pink, yellow or pearl grey. Enokitake mushrooms are tiny, with bud-like caps at the end of long, slender stems.

Shallots

Sometimes called bunching onions, shallots have bulbs that multiply to produce clusters joined at the root end. They tend to be sweeter and much milder than large onions. Indispensable in South-east Asian kitchens, shallots are far more popular than both regular onions and spring onions for everyday use.

Pineapple

Throughout South-east Asia, pineapple is used in sweet and savoury soups. To prepare pineapple, cut off the head of tough leaves, then slice off the thick skin deep enough to remove the 'eyes'. Cut into sizes a required.

Above *Pineapple adds sweetness to tangy hot-and-sour fish soups.*

Mango

Most mangoes are oval in shape, with blushed gold or pink skin. The easiest way to obtain chunks is to cut a lengthways slice off each side of the unpeeled fruit. Score the flesh on each slice with criss-cross lines. Fold these slices inside out and slice off the flesh.

Papaya

Also known as pawpaws, papayas can be small and round, but are usually pear-shaped. Green papayas are used in Indonesia, Malaysia and Thailand.

Lime

These small, green and very sour citrus fruits are used extensively throughout South-east Asia. The most common variety is called Calamansi, and is very popular in the Philippines.

Coconut

A crucial ingredient in many South-east Asian soups, coconut is used in the form of juice, milk or cream. You can buy bags of freshly grated coconut. Warm water is added and the coconut is squeezed until the mixture is cloudy. When strained, this is coconut milk. If left to stand, coconut cream will float to the surface.

Poultry and meat

It is traditional in all South-east Asian cooking for the meat element in a dish to be a relatively small percentage of the whole, with vegetables and noodles or rice making up the major portion. Chicken and duck are immensely popular. Pork is also widely used – like chicken, its flavour blends well with a wide range of ingredients. Lamb is not widely eaten, but there is a burgeoning interest in beef.

Left An oven-ready duck. After roasting, the meat can be used in classic Cambodian dishes such as duck and preserved lime soup.

Chicken

A whole chicken is a sought-after purchase almost everywhere in South-east Asia. The flesh combines happily with a huge variety of ingredients. The breast portion can be sliced or diced for stir-frying, and the bones can be simmered in water to make a stock or soup. In fact, every part of the bird is utilized, including the liver, gizzard, heart and feet. Throughout the East, frugality is a virtue, so one chicken might be used in several dishes. The skill that is exhibited by South-east Asian cooks with the simplest equipment is testament to their creative love of food. Using a cleaver and a small sharp knife, a chicken can be chopped into appropriate portions in no time at all.

Duck

As a symbol of happiness and fidelity, which doubtless contributes to its popularity in South-east Asian cuisine, duck is often central to celebratory meals. It can be served in countless imaginative ways, including being used in small quantities to flavour a substantial broth. When buying duck, look for a bird with a long body and a plump breast. The skin should be unmarked and should look creamy and slightly waxy. The healthiest way of cooking duck breast fillets is to steam them for about an hour, having first removed the skin. The meat can then be sliced and moistened with a little of the water from the steamer.

Pork

This is as popular as chicken in many parts of South-east Asia. Like chicken, it blends beautifully with a wide range of ingredients, from vegetables to shellfish, and is equally at home with salted and pickled foods. Wherever there are Muslim communities, however, pork is off limits, and either beef or lamb is served instead. This is the case throughout Malaysia, the only exception being the Nonya style of cooking. This came about because of the intermarriage of Chinese merchant men with Malayan women, who then started to cook pork dishes for their husbands.

Right
A whole raw chicken. In South-east Asia, every part of the chicken is used – even the feet.

Above *Lean leg steaks, fillet and spare ribs are the preferred cuts of pork.*

Nonya cooking is popular in Singapore, the west coast of Malaysia around Malacca and on the island of Penang.

Pork seldom features in Indonesian cuisine, except where cooked by members of the Chinese communities on the thousands of islands of the archipelago. Bali is an exception.

The population of this island is mainly Hindu, and therefore pork is permissible and widely used. Throughout South-east Asia, therefore, the choice of meat is greatly influenced by religious beliefs and habits.

Choose fillets that are pale pink all over. The flesh should be fairly firm and slightly moist to the touch. Avoid any meat with discoloured areas. To prepare pork fillet, pull away the membrane that surrounds the meat, removing any fat at the same time. The sinew, which looks like a tougher strip of membrane, must be sliced away. The meat can then be cut into thin shreds so that it responds to really quick cooking over high heat, which is economical in the use of fuel. Spare ribs or belly pork can also be used, the meat often being cooked for so long that it forms a luscious jelly-like mixture.

Beef

In much of Thailand and South-east Asia, the cow was for many centuries regarded solely as a beast of burden, thus too precious to be slaughtered for food. Today, however, beef consumption is on the increase. When buying beef, look for deep red meat. For slow-cooked dishes, a generous marbling of fat is required, but if the meat is to be stir-fried, a leaner cut such as fillet (tenderloin) or rump (round) steak should be used. Beef shanks or brisket are suitable for making soup stocks.

Below *When preparing beef for stir-frying, choose lean meat such as rump steak, and cut off any visible fat. The resulting thin strips will cook quickly.*

How to joint a chicken
This method will give you eight good-sized pieces of chicken.

1 Place the chicken breast side up on a chopping board. Ease one of the legs away from the body, and using a sharp knife make an incision to reveal the ball of the thighbone as you pull the leg further away from the body. When the thigh socket is visible, cut through the bone to release the drumstick and thigh in one piece. Repeat with the other leg.

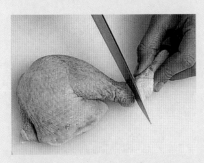

2 Trim off the end of the leg bone, then locate the knee joint and cut the leg portion in half at this joint. Repeat with the other chicken leg.

3 Cut through the breastbone so that the carcass is in two halves. Cut and separate each breast and wing from the backbone.

4 Cut both of the wing and breast pieces into two portions.

Cook's tips
• Use the backbone to make stock, adding onion, celery and a piece of bruised root ginger, if appropriate.
• If more pieces of chicken are required, say for stir-fries, the portions can be further divided. Deft Asian cooks will cut the breast and wing portions into as many as ten pieces, the legs into four pieces and the thighs into six pieces.

Fish and shellfish

Since most of South-east Asia's populations are coastal or island-based, fish and shellfish are extremely important ingredients throughout the regions. The many coastal waters, rivers and lakes provide an abundant harvest.

Carp

This freshwater fish is widely farmed in South-east Asia. It has meaty, moist flesh that can taste a little muddy to those unfamiliar with the distinctive flavour. When buying carp, ask the fishmonger to remove the scales and strong dorsal fins.

Cod

A handsome fish with greenish bronze skin dappled with yellow, cod can vary significantly in size. When properly cooked, the flesh is moist and will break into large flakes. It is excellent in soups, but only add the cubes of pearly white fish at the very end of cooking, so that they keep their shape.

Above *Fresh cod fillets are used in light soups such as Chinese fish ball soup.*

Mackerel

This is a much-loved fish throughout South-east Asia, especially the coastal regions. The dark grey body has silver stripes and usually comes in at around 30cm/12in in length, and it is relatively inexpensive compared to carp. It is an oily fish with soft, pinkish flesh, and is excellent in a laksa or a Thai fish soup.

Grey mullet

This fish has dark stripes along the back, thick scales and a heavy head. The flesh is soft and rather coarse, but responds well to distinctive flavours.

Sea bass

Characterized by the delicate flavour of its flesh, sea bass is enjoyed throughout South-east Asia. The family of sea bass also includes the

Left *(from top) Freshwater carp, mackerel and grey mullet.*

Above *Sea bass provides both substance and delicate flavour in a Filipino fish soup.*

groupers (sometimes called garoupas). It is silver in colour, with a dark back and white underbelly. The flesh is delicate in flavour and holds its shape when cooked. The fish can be cut into fillets or steaks before being cooked. It is expensive, but worth it.

Below *Red snapper forms the basis of Vietnamese hot and sour fish soup.*

Snapper

The red snapper is perhaps the best known, but there other colours too, such as grey, silver, and even a silver-spotted grey. The red colour is quite distinctive. The fish has large eyes and strong dorsal fins which should be removed before cooking. The flesh is well flavoured, and is often used in Vietnamese dishes.

Squid

South-east Asian cooks are very fond of squid. In the West, this cephalopod usually comes ready-cleaned, but if you should come across it in the unprepared state, here is what to do.

Pull the tentacles out from the body sac. Squeeze the tentacle in the centre gently to remove the hard central bone or 'beak'. Trim the tentacles from the head and set aside. Using your fingers, pull the quill and innards from the body cavity and discard. Pull off the mottled outer skin; it should come away quite easily. Wash the squid well inside and out. If the squid is to be stir-fried, slit the sac from top to bottom and turn it inside out. Flatten it on a board

Below *Squid can be used fresh or dried, and is delicious in light, aromatic soups.*

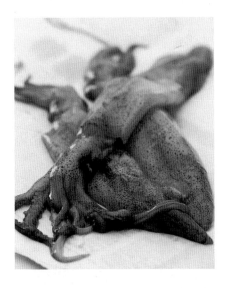

Left *Prawns feature in countless South-east Asian soup recipes. In some dishes you can leave the shells on, to give extra flavour and texture.*

and score the inside surface lightly with a knife, pressing just hard enough to make a criss-cross pattern. Cut lengthways into ribbons. These will curl when cooked.

The cardinal rule with squid is to either cook it very quickly, or simmer it for a long time. Anything in between will result in seafood that is tough and rubbery.

Prawns and shrimp

If you ask for shrimp in Britain, then you will be given tiny crustaceans, while in the United States the term is used to describe the larger shellfish that the British refer to as prawns. However, South-east Asian cooks use both words fairly indiscriminately, so check what the recipe requires. Buy raw shellfish whenever possible, then cook it yourself. This applies to fresh and frozen mixed seafood. If the shellfish are frozen, you should thaw them slowly and pat them dry before cooking.

Cockles

These are small saltwater clams, and inside each one lies a morsel of delicate flesh and its coral. They are a key ingredient in a seafood laksa, and should be added at the last minute, after being shelled.

Preparing prawns/shrimp

Using this 'butterfly' method will help prawns or shrimp to cook quickly and curl attractively.

1 Remove the heads and body shells, but leave the tails intact. Pull out the intestinal cords using a pair of tweezers.

2 Make a cut through the belly of each prawn.

3 Gently open out the two halves of the prawn so that they look like butterfly wings.

Tofu

Made from soya beans, tofu (also widely known as beancurd) is popular throughout South-east Asia and one of the cheapest sources of protein in the world. Highly nutritious and low in fat and sugar, it is a much healthier food than either meat or fish, at a fraction of the cost. The nutritional value of tofu cannot be stressed too highly. As a vegetable protein, it contains the eight essential amino acids plus vitamins A and B. It is free from cholesterol, and is regarded as an excellent food for anyone with heart disease or high blood pressure. In addition, it is very easy to digest, so is an ideal food for infants, invalids and the elderly.

Tofu is a very versatile ingredient and, depending upon the texture, it can be cooked by almost every conceivable method, including stir-frying, steaming and poaching. It can be used with a vast array of ingredients, both sweet and savoury. It is freely used as a meat replacement.

Although tofu is bland, it picks up the flavours of other foods when marinated. It is important to cook it with strongly flavoured seasonings such as garlic, ginger, spring onions (scallions), chillies, soy sauce, oyster sauce, shrimp paste or sesame oil. Tofu tastes very good with meat. It is often cooked with either pork or beef, but seldom with chicken. It also goes well with fish and shellfish.

Types of tofu

Two basic types of fresh tofu are widely available: soft or silken tofu; and a firm type called momen. Both kinds are creamy white in colour and are either packed in water or sold in vacuum packs.

Tofu can be used in a variety of ways in South-east Asian cooking – cut into cubes and stir-fried, or deep-fried in hot oil in a wok, for example. It can significantly enhance the flavour of a dish. When it is cooked in hot oil, it puffs up and turns golden brown,

Above *(clockwise from top) Deep-fried tofu, silken tofu, and cubes of fresh tofu. All these absorb the flavours of the ingredients with which they are cooked.*

Above *Always use a sharp knife when cutting firm tofu, as a blunt knife will squash the tofu and cause it to crumble. Place a block of tofu on a clean chopping board and cut it into slices about 2cm/³⁄₄in thick, or the required size for the recipe. If the recipe calls for cubes, cut the slices in half, and then into cubes.*

the flavour intensifies and the texture becomes chewy. Cubes of deep-fried tofu are sold in Asian markets. They should be stored in the refrigerator and used within three days.

The quality of fresh tofu is largely dependent upon the water used to make it. Good-quality tofu should smell fresh, with a faint, pleasant 'beany' aroma. Soft or silken tofu is appropriate for soups, since its light and delicate texture means that it will disintegrate if handled roughly. Firm tofu is popular for everyday use. Although it has been lightly pressed and is more robust than silken tofu, it still needs to be handled with care. Having been cut to the required size and shape – cubes, strips, slices or triangles – the pieces are usually blanched in boiling water or briefly shallow-fried in oil. This hardens them and prevents them from disintegrating when stir-fried or braised.

Rice

Needless to say, rice is immensely important throughout South-east Asia. It is a central staple, and is served with many dishes. When Thais are called to the table, the invitation *kin khao* literally translates as 'a time to eat rice'. In Malaysia, Indonesia and Singapore, the phrase 'to eat rice' alludes to basic sustenance, whether rice is involved or not. All the other foods that make up a meal – meat, fish and vegetables – are regarded as accompaniments.

The average South-east Asian eats 158kg/350lb of rice every year, which is almost 250g/9oz per day, but spread over two or three main meals. White rice is generally preferred over brown varieties.

Jasmine rice
Very popular in South-east Asia, jasmine rice is a delicately scented variety that is used as a staple with all meals. When properly cooked with the requisite amount of water, it is fluffy. As the name suggests, jasmine

Below Jasmine rice or 'fragrant rice' has tender, aromatic grains, and is popular throughout central and southern Thailand and much of South-east Asia.

rice has a delicate aroma. The flavour is slightly nutty. Most of the rice eaten in the Indo-Chinese countries comes from a region between central and north-eastern Thailand, where the soil is a combination of clay and sand. Newly harvested rice from this region is prized for the delicate texture of the grains. In fact, jasmine rice has become synonymous with Thailand, and most of what you buy in Asian stores is this particular type. The common reference to jasmine rice is 'fragrant rice'.

Long grain rice
The simplest method for identifying rice is by the length of the grain, which can be long, medium or short. Long grain rice has grains that are three or four times as long as they are wide. When cooked, the individual grains separate. The most common variety used in South-east Asian cooking is white – this has been fully milled, and all of the bran and outer coating

Below Long grain rice can be used in a variety of soup recipes. The white variety is often described as 'polished', as it has a smooth and glossy appearance.

Above *Rice is best cooked using the absorption method. Cook the rice with water in a tightly covered pan, then leave for 5 minutes until tender, before serving.*

have been removed. The grains are white and slightly shiny, a feature often described by the expression 'polished'.

Short grain rice
This type of rice absorbs liquid, becoming soft and sticky in the process. It is almost as broad as it is long, and is sometimes described as 'round grain'. The grains stick together when cooked.

Below Short grain rice is a large, plump grain. As the rice cooks, it dissolves in the stock that is constantly added, giving the finished soup a creamy texture.

Noodles and wrappers

Second only to rice in importance in the South-east Asian diet, noodles and wrappers are cooked in a vast number of ways. For the local populations, soup noodles are easily the most popular dish. Wrappers are made from egg and wheat flour, and are used to wrap around a filling. They can be steamed, boiled or deep-fried.

There are many varieties of noodles used in South-east Asian cooking. Most can be bought fresh, but it is more likely that you will find them dried. They come in several sizes, from tiny transparent threads to large sheets. Many are made from rice, which serves to further emphasize the importance of the grain in the South-east Asian diet. Others are based on wheat flour or flour made from ground mung beans.

Rice noodles

Both fresh and dried rice noodles are available. Fresh noodles are highly perishable, and they must be cooked

Below Rice vermicelli is thin and wiry, and sold in bundles. It needs to be soaked in warm water before use.

as soon as possible after purchase. Rice noodles come in a wide range of shapes and widths, from fine vermicelli to thick, round rice noodle nests.

Rice vermicelli are a thin form of rice noodles, particularly popular in Thailand. They are usually sold dried, and they cook almost instantly in hot liquid, provided the noodles are first soaked in warm water.

Rice sticks are flat rice noodles used in Malaysia and Vietnam. They are sold both dried and fresh, although the latter form is more popular. When fresh, they tend to be rather sticky and need to be separated before being cooked.

Rice noodle nests are thick, round noodles. A Thai speciality, they are also known by the name of *khanom chine* or Chinese noodles. They are white, and the strands are a little thicker than spaghetti. At most markets in Thailand, nests of these noodles are a familiar sight. They are sold freshly cooked. You can buy them by the hundred, and you should allow four or five nests per person. Buy the cheaper ones, because they taste better even though they are not as white as the more expensive ones.

Fresh noodle nests are highly perishable, so, even though they are cooked, it makes sense to buy them early in the day, and steam them again when you get them home.

Preparing rice noodles is a simple matter. They need only to be soaked in hot water for a few minutes to soften them before serving. Add the noodles to

Above *Rice sticks are a form of flat rice noodle not unlike Italian tagliatelle or linguine. They are available in several widths, starting at around 2mm/^{1}/$_{16}$in.*

a large bowl of just-boiled water and leave for 5–10 minutes, or until they soften, stirring occasionally to separate the strands. Their dry weight will usually double after soaking, so 115g/4oz dry noodles will produce about 225g/8oz after soaking.

Rice sticks puff up and become wonderfully crisp when they are deep-fried. Just a few deep-fried noodles sprinkled over a dish of boiled or reconstituted noodles will enhance the flavour wonderfully.

To prepare deep-fried rice noodles, place the noodles in a large mixing bowl and soak in cold water for 15 minutes. Drain them and lay them on kitchen paper to dry. Then heat about 1.2 litres/2 pints/5 cups vegetable oil in a large, high-sided

Above *Egg noodles are made from wheat flour, egg and water. They are firmer and denser than rice noodles. Dried varieties must be soaked in hot water before cooking, and fresh ones come in nests that must be shaken loose before use.*

frying pan or wok to 180°C/350°F. To test if the oil is ready, carefully drop in a couple of noodle strands. If they puff and curl up immediately, the oil is hot enough. Very carefully, add a handful of dry noodles to the hot oil. As soon as they puff up, after about 2 seconds, flip them over with a long-handled strainer and cook for 2 seconds more. Transfer to a large baking sheet lined with kitchen paper and leave to cool. When the fried noodles are cold, they can be transferred to a sealed plastic bag and will stay crisp for about two days.

Egg noodles

These noodles owe their yellow colour to the egg used in their manufacture. Many are made by local manufacturers and sold in South-east Asian supermarkets. They come in both flat and round shapes, and are sold dried or fresh. When bought fresh in nests, they must be shaken loose before being

Above *Cellophane or mung bean thread noodles are as thin as rice vermicelli, and white in colour. They turn transparent when cooked, taking on the appearance of cellophane or glass, and they absorb the flavour of surrounding ingredients.*

cooked. Very thin noodles are known as egg thread noodles. The flat type are generally used for soups.

Egg noodles freeze well, provided they are correctly wrapped. Thaw them thoroughly before using in soup dishes.

Cooking noodles

Both dried and fresh noodles have to be cooked in boiling water before use – or soaked in warm water until pliable. How long for depends on the type of noodle, their thickness and whether or not the noodles are going to be cooked again in a soup. As a rule, once they have been soaked, dried noodles require about 3 minutes' cooking, while fresh ones will often be ready in less than a minute, and may need to be rinsed under cold water to prevent them from overcooking.

They should be cooked in boiling water for 4–5 minutes, or according to the instructions on the packet. Then drain and serve.

Cellophane noodles

These thin, wiry noodles are also called mung bean thread noodles. They are the same size as ordinary egg noodles, but they are transparent, resembling strips of cellophane or glass. They are only available dried. They do not have much taste, but they absorb other flavours; they are often used to add texture and starch to soups. Soak them in hot water for 10–15 minutes to soften them, then drain and cut into shorter strands.

Won ton wrappers

Originally Chinese, these thin yellow pastry squares are made from egg and wheat flour, and can be bought fresh or frozen. Fresh wrappers will last for about five days, double-wrapped and stored in the refrigerator. Simply peel off the number you require. Frozen wrappers should be thawed before use.

Below *Won ton wrappers are small square sheets rolled from egg noodle dough. They are available in packets from South-east Asian food markets.*

Herbs and spices

The principal herbs and spices favoured in South-east Asia have made a tremendous contribution to global cuisine. Ingredients such as fresh ginger, lemon grass and kaffir lime now feature on menus the world over – not just in recipes that reflect their origin, but also in fusion food.

Basil
Many types of basil are grown in Thailand and throughout Indonesia, each with a slightly different appearance, flavour and use. Thai basil, or *horapha*, has a sweet, anise flavour. Holy basil, or *kaphrao*, has a pronounced lemon scent infused with cloves. Indonesian basil is variously called *daun selasih* or *kemangi*, and is very similar to the Thai cultivars, but with minty top notes.

Coriander/cilantro
The entire coriander plant is used in South-east Asian cooking. The fresh, delicate leaves are used as garnishes, and the roots and stems are crushed and used as flavourings.

Left *Lemon grass imparts a distinctive flavour to soups from all regions of South-east Asia.*

Lemon grass
A perennial tufted plant with a bulbous base, lemon grass looks like a plump spring onion (scallion). When the stalk is cut or bruised, the lively citrus aroma becomes evident. The stalk is usually kept whole, bruised, and then cooked slowly in liquid until it releases its flavour and is removed.

Kaffir lime leaves
These leaves are not from true limes, but belong to a subspecies of the citrus family. Native to South-east Asia, they have green knobbly skins. The fruit is not used as it yields very little juice, but the leaves are most highly prized in soups. Kaffir lime leaves are synonymous with Thai and Indonesian cooking.

Above *Garlic cloves can be chopped and added to soups, or alternatively ground into a paste using a mortar and pestle.*

Garlic
Often used with spring onions (scallions) and ginger, garlic is a vital ingredient in South-east Asian dishes. The most common variety has a white skin, a fairly distinctive aroma and a hint of sweetness.

Ginger
Valued not just as an aromatic but also for its medicinal qualities, ginger is used throughout South-east Asia.

Below *Thai basil.*

Below *Fresh coriander.*

Below *Kaffir lime leaves.*

Above *Fresh root ginger should be peeled and chopped before adding to soups.*

When young, ginger is juicy and tender, with a sharp flavour suggestive of citrus. At this stage it can easily be sliced, chopped or pounded to a paste. Older roots are tougher and may need to be peeled and grated. Pickled ginger is delicious, and is often used in soups.

Galangal

Slightly harder than ginger, galangal is used in much the same way. When young, the skin is creamy white with pink sprouts, and the flavour is lemony. As galangal matures, the flavour intensifies and becomes more peppery. It is integral to Indonesian, Malaysian and Singapore cooking.

Below *Galangal.*

Turmeric

A member of the ginger family, turmeric is a smaller root with an intense orange colour, and is available fresh or as a powder, essential to many Indonesian and Malaysian soups. It provides both colour and a strong fragrance. It has to be peeled before use, and be sure to wear rubber gloves, because the colour is indelible when it gets on to clothing.

Tamarind

Called *asam* in Indonesia and Malaysia, tamarind comes in paste form or as dry pods. They yield a sour liquid not unlike lemon juice, and are indispensable in soups. You can buy the juice in a bottle.

Chillies

Although they did not originate in South-east Asia, chillies have been embraced fervently throughout the

Below *Turmeric powder.*

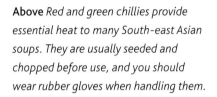

Above *Red and green chillies provide essential heat to many South-east Asian soups. They are usually seeded and chopped before use, and you should wear rubber gloves when handling them.*

region. All other South-east Asian cuisines would be pale shadows of themselves without these fiery pods. They are especially essential in a variety of soups. Much appreciated for their flavour and fire, especially in Thai and Indonesian dishes, they range from tiny varieties called bird chillies to very fat ones. Be careful when you handle chillies. They contain a substance called capsaicin, which is a powerful irritant. If this comes into contact with delicate skin or the eyes, it can cause considerable pain. Wear rubber gloves when handling chillies, or wash your hands thoroughly in hot soapy water afterwards.

Below *Tamarind pods.*

Flavourings and sauces

There are many different flavourings and sauces that can be used to give South-east Asian soups their distinctive character, taste and aroma. Here are a few essentials you will need.

Pastes

Most spice pastes use a common blend of ground ingredients. Known as *sambal* in Indonesia, Malaysia and Singapore, they draw on the range of fresh and dried herbs.

Curry paste is often used in Thai cooking, and is made from shrimp paste, chillies, onions or shallots, garlic, lemon grass, galangal and coriander (cilantro) root. It can be either red or green, depending on the colour of the chillies.

Magic paste is the name given to a Thai paste that is a mixture of crushed garlic, white pepper and coriander.

Chilli paste consists of a blend of chilli peppers, garlic, oil and salt, and gives heat to South-east Asian soups.

Below *Red curry paste.*

Above *Chilli paste.*

Shrimp paste, made from ground prawns (shrimp) fermented in brine, is universally used throughout South-east Asia, and is essential in many soup recipes. It is quite pungent and has to be stored in airtight containers either in a larder or the fridge. It is usually sold in wrapped blocks or in jars, and can be hard or soft, depending on its origin. It is known by different names in each region of South-east Asia (see panel).

Below *Green curry paste.*

Regional names for shrimp paste
belacan (Malaysia)
terasi (Indonesia)
kapi (Thailand, Cambodia, Laos)
ngapi (Myanmar)
mam ruoc (Vietnam)

Tamarind paste is a very dark substance made from boiled-down tamarind fruits. It is often used in Thai recipes, and flavours the soup with sour notes.

Oils

Groundnut (peanut) oil is a mild-tasting oil derived from peanuts, and is widely used in South-east Asian soup recipes, both for cooking and to add flavour.

Sesame oil is used to give added aroma to soups; it has a distinctive fragrance, and only a little is needed for good effect.

Below *Shrimp paste.*

Above *Groundnut oil.*

Chilli oil is important for giving the requisite colour to soups.

Vegetable oil is used for frying ingredients such as shallots, onions and garlic, and also for deep-frying.

Vinegars

Rice wine vinegar is the preferred choice of South-east Asian cooks, because it is an inexpensive by-product of rice.

Coconut vinegar is somewhat esoteric compared to other types, as it is not widely available. Made mostly in South India and the Philippines, it is the result of allowing coconut water to ferment over time. It is of a mild, intoxicating nature.

Above *Rice wine vinegars.*

Sauces

Soy sauce covers a rather wide spectrum, and ranges from thin, light soy to sweet, treacle-like ones that many Indonesian dishes rely on. Basically, soy sauce is to the East what salt is to the West. Dark soy imparts a nice ebony colour, and light soy is simply a salting agent, but has more flavour than table salt.

Fish sauce is the prime salting agent in most South-east Asian countries, especially Thailand, Vietnam and Laos. It is more pungent than Chinese soy sauce, and marries well with herbs such as kaffir lime leaves and lime juice. It can also be blended with chillies and chopped nuts. It is known as *patis* in the Philippines, and *nam pla* in Cambodia.

Hoisin sauce is the result of adding sugar to yellow bean paste for its required sweetness.

Below *Fish sauce.*

Above *(from top) Dark soy sauce and light soy sauce.*

Making stocks

A good stock forms the basis for flavoursome South-east Asian soups. It is worth taking the time to make your own, to give your finished dishes a depth of taste. Here is how to make meat, seafood and vegetable stocks.

Meat stock: Take 1kg/2¼lb pork ribs and simmer in 1.2 litres/ 2 pints/5 cups water for a good hour. Strain and allow to chill. When cold, skim of any solid, white fat, and you have a clear stock. Vietnamese cooks use beef ribs for their hearty stocks in beef noodles.

Seafood stock: The same goes for seafood stock, in which good use can be made of salmon heads. A quantity of 500g/1¼lb fish needs 1 litre/1¾ pints/4 cups water, simmered for 30 minutes. Strain and use as needed. When using shellfish such as prawns (shrimp) bought on the shell, do not discard the shells, but add them to the same stock. This imparts an even richer taste.

Vegetable stock: This is best made with root vegetables such as mooli, celery, cabbage and the stalk ends of greens such as spring greens (collards), pak choi (bok choy) and any other kind of greens. Cut up the vegetables into small pieces, and allow 500g/1¼lb vegetables to 1 litre/1¾ pints/4 cups water. Simmer for 30–40 minutes until the vegetables are completely soft. Strain through a colander and press down to extract every drop of liquid.

THAILAND

In Thailand, soups are not seen as curtain-raisers, but are served throughout the meal, providing the palate with tastes and textures that complement or contrast with those in more dominant dishes. You may choose to serve any of these soups solo, as a light lunch or supper dish, or as a prelude to a dinner party, but however and whenever you place them before your guests, treats such as Cellophane Noodle Soup and Northern Prawn and Squash Soup are certain to prove popular.

Hot and sweet vegetable and tofu soup

This interesting combination of hot, sweet and sour flavours makes for a soothing, nutritious soup. It takes only minutes to prepare, as the spinach and silken tofu are simply placed in bowls and then covered with the flavoured hot stock.

1 Heat the stock in a large pan, then add the red curry paste. Stir constantly over a medium heat until the paste has dissolved.

2 Add the lime leaves, sugar and soy sauce and bring to the boil.

3 Add the lime juice and carrot to the pan. Reduce the heat and simmer for 5–10 minutes. Place the spinach and tofu in four individual serving bowls and pour the hot stock on top to serve.

Cook's Tip Silken tofu is very soft, smooth and creamy, and has a high water content. Take it out of the package and drain off excess water before using.

Serves four

1.2 litres/2 pints/5 cups vegetable stock

5–10ml/1–2 tsp Thai red curry paste

2 kaffir lime leaves, torn

40g/1½oz/3 tbsp palm sugar or light muscovado (brown) sugar

30ml/2 tbsp soy sauce

juice of 1 lime

1 carrot, cut into thin batons

50g/2oz baby spinach leaves, any coarse stalks removed

225g/8oz block silken tofu, diced

Energy 103kcal/434kJ; Protein 5.5g; Carbohydrate 13.3g, of which sugars 12.8g; Fat 3.5g, of which saturates 0.4g; Cholesterol 0mg; Calcium 320mg; Fibre 0.7g; Sodium 769mg.

Mixed vegetable soup

Serves four

30ml/2 tbsp groundnut (peanut) oil

15ml/1 tbsp magic paste
(see Cook's Tip)

90g/3½oz Savoy cabbage or
Chinese leaves (Chinese cabbage),
finely shredded

90g/3½oz mooli (daikon),
finely diced

1 medium cauliflower, coarsely
chopped

4 celery sticks, coarsely chopped

1.2 litres/2 pints/5 cups
vegetable stock

130g/4½oz fried tofu, cut into
2.5cm/1in cubes

5ml/1 tsp palm sugar or light
muscovado (brown) sugar

45ml/3 tbsp light soy sauce

In Thailand, this type of soup is usually made in large quantities and then reheated for consumption over several days. If you would like to do the same, double or treble the quantities. Chill any leftover soup rapidly, and reheat thoroughly before serving.

1 Heat the groundnut oil in a large, heavy pan or wok. Add the magic paste and cook over a low heat, stirring frequently, until it gives off its aroma.

2 Add the shredded Savoy cabbage or Chinese leaves, mooli, cauliflower and celery. Pour in the vegetable stock, increase the heat to medium and bring to the boil, stirring occasionally. Gently stir in the tofu cubes.

3 Add the sugar and soy sauce. Reduce the heat and simmer for 15 minutes, until the vegetables are cooked and tender. Taste and add a little more soy sauce if needed. Serve hot.

Cook's Tip Magic paste is a mixture of crushed garlic, white pepper and coriander (cilantro). Look for it at Thai markets.

Energy 134kcal/554kJ; Protein 7.7g; Carbohydrate 7.5g, of which sugars 6.6g; Fat 8.2g, of which saturates 1.5g; Cholesterol 0mg; Calcium 220mg; Fibre 3g; Sodium 1044mg.

Omelette soup

A very satisfying soup that is quick and easy to prepare. It is versatile, too, in that you can vary the vegetables according to what is seasonally available.

1 Put the egg in a bowl and beat lightly with a fork. Heat the oil in a small frying pan until it is hot, but not smoking. Pour in the egg and swirl the pan so that it coats the base evenly. Cook over a medium heat until the omelette has set and the underside is golden. Slide it out of the pan and roll it up like a pancake. Slice into 5mm/¼in rounds and set aside for the garnish.

2 Put the stock into a large pan. Add the carrots and cabbage and bring to the boil. Reduce the heat and simmer for 5 minutes, then add the soy sauce, granulated sugar and pepper.

3 Stir well, then pour into warmed bowls. Lay a few omelette rounds on the surface of each portion, and complete the garnish with the coriander leaves.

Serves four

1 egg

15ml/1 tbsp groundnut (peanut) oil

900ml/1½ pints/3¾ cups vegetable stock

2 large carrots, finely diced

4 outer leaves Savoy cabbage, shredded

30ml/2 tbsp soy sauce

2.5ml/½ tsp granulated sugar

2.5ml/½ tsp ground black pepper

fresh coriander (cilantro) leaves, to garnish

Energy 68kcal/283kJ; Protein 2.7g; Carbohydrate 3.9g, of which sugars 3.6g; Fat 4.7g, of which saturates 1g; Cholesterol 55mg; Calcium 28mg; Fibre 1.1g; Sodium 772mg.

Serves four

4 large dried shiitake mushrooms

15g/½oz dried lily buds

½ cucumber, coarsely chopped

2 garlic cloves, halved

90g/3½oz white cabbage, chopped

1.2 litres/2 pints/5 cups boiling water

115g/4oz cellophane noodles

30ml/2 tbsp soy sauce

15ml/1 tbsp palm sugar or light muscovado (brown) sugar

90g/3½oz block silken tofu, diced

fresh coriander (cilantro) leaves, to garnish

Cellophane noodle soup

The noodles used in this soup go by various names: glass noodles, cellophane noodles, bean thread or transparent noodles. They are especially valued for their brittle texture.

1 Soak the shiitake mushrooms in warm water for 30 minutes. In a separate bowl, soak the dried lily buds in warm water, also for 30 minutes.

2 Meanwhile, put the cucumber, garlic and cabbage in a food processor and process to a smooth paste. Scrape the mixture into a large pan and add the measured boiling water.

3 Bring to the boil, then reduce the heat and cook for 2 minutes, stirring occasionally. Strain this stock into another pan, return to a low heat and bring to simmering point.

4 Drain the lily buds, rinse under cold running water, then drain again. Cut off any hard ends. Add the lily buds to the stock with the noodles, soy sauce and sugar and cook for 5 minutes more.

5 Strain the mushroom soaking liquid into the soup. Discard the mushroom stems, then slice the caps. Divide them and the tofu among four bowls. Pour the soup over, garnish and serve.

Energy 143kcal/598kJ; Protein 4.1g; Carbohydrate 28.3g, of which sugars 4.7g; Fat 1.2g, of which saturates 0.1g; Cholesterol 0mg; Calcium 135mg; Fibre 0.9g; Sodium 8mg.

Galangal, chicken and coconut soup

This aromatic soup – *tom kha gai* – is rich with coconut milk, and intensely flavoured with galangal, lemon grass and kaffir lime leaves.

1 Cut off the lower 5cm/2in from each lemon grass stalk and chop it finely. Bruise the remaining pieces of stalk. Bring the coconut milk and chicken stock to the boil in a large pan over a medium heat. Add the chopped and bruised lemon grass, the galangal, peppercorns and half the kaffir lime leaves, reduce the heat to low and simmer gently for 10 minutes. Strain the soup into a clean pan.

2 Return the soup to a low heat, then stir in the chicken strips, mushrooms and corn. Simmer gently, stirring occasionally, for 5–7 minutes, or until the chicken is cooked.

3 Stir in the lime juice and fish sauce, then add the remaining lime leaves. Ladle into warm bowls and serve, garnished with chillies, spring onions and coriander leaves.

Serves four to six

4 lemon grass stalks, roots trimmed

2 x 400ml/14fl oz cans coconut milk

475ml/16fl oz/2 cups chicken stock

2.5cm/1in piece fresh galangal, peeled and thinly sliced

10 black peppercorns, crushed

10 kaffir lime leaves, torn

300g/11oz skinless, boneless chicken breast portions, cut into thin strips

115g/4oz/1 cup button (white) mushrooms, halved if large

50g/2oz/½ cup baby corn cobs, quartered lengthways

60ml/4 tbsp fresh lime juice

45ml/3 tbsp Thai fish sauce

chopped fresh red chillies, spring onions (scallions) and fresh coriander (cilantro) leaves, to garnish

Hot-and-sour prawn soup

This is a classic Thai seafood soup – *tom yam kung* – and it is one of the most popular and best-known soups from Thailand.

1 Peel the prawns, reserving the shells. Devein the prawns and set aside.

2 Rinse the shells under cold water, then put them in a large pan with the stock or water. Bring to the boil.

3 Bruise the lemon grass stalks and add them to the stock with half the lime leaves. Simmer gently for 5–6 minutes, until the stock is fragrant.

4 Strain the stock, return it to the clean pan and reheat. Add the drained mushrooms and the prawns, then cook until the prawns turn pink.

5 Stir the fish sauce, lime juice, spring onion, coriander, chillies and the remaining lime leaves into the soup. Taste and adjust the seasoning if necessary. The soup should be sour, salty, spicy and hot.

Serves four to six

450g/1lb raw king prawns (jumbo shrimp), thawed if frozen

1 litre/1¾ pints/4 cups chicken stock or water

3 lemon grass stalks, roots trimmed

10 kaffir lime leaves, torn in half

225g/8oz can straw mushrooms, drained

45ml/3 tbsp Thai fish sauce

60ml/4 tbsp fresh lime juice

30ml/2 tbsp chopped spring onion (scallion)

15ml/1 tbsp fresh coriander (cilantro) leaves

4 fresh red chillies, seeded and thinly sliced

salt and ground black pepper

Top: Energy 134kcal/571kJ; Protein 19.8g; Carbohydrate 10.7g, of which sugars 10.4g; Fat 1.7g, of which saturates 0.7g; Cholesterol 53mg; Calcium 66mg; Fibre 0.5g; Sodium 887mg.

Bottom: Energy 103kcal/434kJ; Protein 21.5g; Carbohydrate 1.1g, of which sugars 0.7g; Fat 1.4g, of which saturates 0.2g; Cholesterol 219mg; Calcium 100mg; Fibre 0.8g; Sodium 892mg.

Chiang Mai noodle soup

Nowadays a signature dish of the city of Chiang Mai, this delicious noodle soup originated in Burma, now called Myanmar, which lies only a little to the north. It is also the Thai equivalent of the famous Malaysian laksa.

1 Pour about one-third of the coconut milk into a large, heavy pan or wok. Bring to the boil over a medium heat, stirring frequently with a wooden spoon until the milk separates.

2 Add the curry paste and ground turmeric, stir to mix completely and cook until the mixture is fragrant.

3 Add the chunks of chicken and toss over the heat for about 2 minutes, making sure that all the chunks are thoroughly coated with the paste.

4 Add the remaining coconut milk, the chicken stock, fish sauce and soy sauce. Season with salt and pepper to taste. Bring to simmering point, stirring frequently, then lower the heat and cook gently for 7–10 minutes. Remove from the heat and stir in lime juice to taste.

5 Reheat the fresh egg noodles in boiling water, drain and divide among four to six warmed bowls. Divide the chunks of chicken among the bowls and ladle in the hot soup. Top each serving with spring onions, chillies, shallots, pickled mustard leaves, fried garlic, coriander leaves and a fried noodle nest, if using. Serve immediately.

Serves four to six

600ml/1 pint/2½ cups coconut milk

30ml/2 tbsp Thai red curry paste

5ml/1 tsp ground turmeric

450g/1lb chicken thighs, boned and cut into bitesize chunks

600ml/1 pint/2½ cups chicken stock

60ml/4 tbsp Thai fish sauce

15ml/1 tbsp dark soy sauce

juice of ½–1 lime

450g/1lb fresh egg noodles, blanched briefly in boiling water

salt and ground black pepper

To garnish

3 spring onions (scallions), chopped

4 fresh red chillies, chopped

4 shallots, chopped

60ml/4 tbsp sliced pickled mustard leaves, rinsed

30ml/2 tbsp fried sliced garlic

coriander (cilantro) leaves

4–6 fried noodle nests (optional)

Energy 606kcal/2569kJ; Protein 39.5g; Carbohydrate 88.7g, of which sugars 10.1g; Fat 12.9g, of which saturates 3.7g; Cholesterol 135mg; Calcium 84mg; Fibre 3.3g; Sodium 1111mg.

Serves two

900ml/1½ pints/3¾ cups vegetable stock

200g/7oz/1¾ cups cooked rice

225g/8oz minced (ground) pork

15ml/1 tbsp Thai fish sauce

2 heads pickled garlic, finely chopped

1 celery stick, finely diced

salt and ground black pepper

To garnish

30ml/2 tbsp groundnut (peanut) oil

4 garlic cloves, thinly sliced

4 small red shallots, finely sliced

Rice porridge

Originating in China, this dish has now spread throughout the whole of South-east Asia, and is loved for its comforting blandness. It is invariably served with a few strongly flavoured accompaniments.

1 Make the garnishes by heating the groundnut oil in a frying pan and cooking the garlic and shallots over a low heat until brown. Drain on kitchen paper and reserve for the soup.

2 Pour the stock into a large pan. Bring to the boil and add the rice. Season the minced pork. Add it by taking small teaspoons and tapping the spoon on the side of the pan so that the meat falls into the soup in small lumps.

3 Stir in the fish sauce and pickled garlic and simmer for 10 minutes, until the pork is cooked. Stir in the celery.

4 Serve the rice porridge in individual warmed bowls. Sprinkle the prepared garlic and shallots on top and season with plenty of ground pepper.

Energy 509kcal/2126kJ; Protein 27.3g; Carbohydrate 37.2g, of which sugars 0.8g; Fat 29g, of which saturates 6.3g; Cholesterol 74mg; Calcium 39mg; Fibre 1.8g; Sodium 86mg.

Smoked mackerel and tomato soup

All the ingredients for this unusual soup are cooked in a single pan, so it's not only quick and easy to prepare, but also reduces the clearing up. Smoked mackerel gives the soup a robust flavour, but this is tempered by the citrus tones in the lemon grass and tamarind.

1 Prepare the smoked mackerel fillets. Remove and discard the skin, if necessary, then chop the flesh into large pieces. Remove any stray bones with your fingers or a pair of tweezers.

2 Cut the tomatoes in half, squeeze out most of the seeds with your fingers, then finely dice the flesh with a sharp knife. Set aside.

3 Pour the stock into a large pan and add the lemon grass, galangal, shallots and garlic. Bring to the boil, reduce the heat and simmer for 15 minutes.

4 Add the fish, tomatoes, chilli flakes, fish sauce, sugar and tamarind juice. Simmer for 4–5 minutes, until the fish and tomatoes are heated through. Serve garnished with chives or spring onions.

Serves four

200g/7oz smoked mackerel fillets

4 tomatoes

1 litre/1¾ pints/4 cups vegetable stock

1 lemon grass stalk, finely chopped

5cm/2in piece fresh galangal, finely diced

4 shallots, finely chopped

2 garlic cloves, finely chopped

2.5ml/½ tsp dried chilli flakes

15ml/1 tbsp Thai fish sauce

5ml/1 tsp palm sugar or light muscovado (brown) sugar

45ml/3 tbsp thick tamarind juice, made by mixing tamarind paste with warm water

small bunch fresh chives or spring onions (scallions), to garnish

Energy 209kcal/868kJ; Protein 10.3g; Carbohydrate 6.6g, of which sugars 6.5g; Fat 15.9g, of which saturates 3.2g; Cholesterol 53mg; Calcium 19mg; Fibre 0.8g; Sodium 681mg.

Serves four to six

450g/1lb pumpkin

2 garlic cloves, crushed

4 shallots, finely chopped

2.5ml/½ tsp shrimp paste

1 lemon grass stalk, chopped

2 fresh green chillies, seeded

15ml/1 tbsp dried shrimp soaked for 10 minutes in warm water to cover

600ml/1 pint/2½ cups chicken stock

600ml/1 pint/2½ cups coconut cream

30ml/2 tbsp Thai fish sauce

5ml/1 tsp granulated sugar

115g/4oz small cooked shelled prawns (shrimp)

salt and ground black pepper

To garnish

2 fresh red chillies, seeded and thinly sliced

10–12 fresh basil leaves

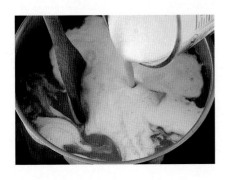

Pumpkin, prawn and coconut soup

The natural sweetness of the pumpkin is heightened by the addition of a little sugar in this lovely looking soup, but this is balanced by the chillies, shrimp paste and dried shrimp. Coconut cream blurs the boundaries beautifully.

1 Peel the pumpkin and cut it into quarters with a sharp knife. Scoop out the seeds with a teaspoon and discard. Cut the flesh into chunks about 2cm/¾in thick and set aside.

2 Put the garlic, shallots, shrimp paste, lemon grass, green chillies and salt to taste in a mortar. Drain the dried shrimp, discarding the soaking liquid, and add them, then use a pestle to grind the mixture into a paste. Alternatively, place all the ingredients in a food processor and process to a paste.

3 Bring the chicken stock to the boil in a large pan. Add the ground paste and stir well to dissolve.

4 Add the pumpkin chunks and bring to a simmer. Simmer for 10–15 minutes, or until the pumpkin is tender.

5 Stir in the coconut cream, then bring the soup back to simmering point. Do not let it boil. Add the fish sauce, sugar and ground black pepper to taste.

6 Add the prawns and cook for a further 2–3 minutes, until they are heated through. Serve in warm soup bowls, garnished with chillies and basil leaves.

Energy 77kcal/328kJ; Protein 6.8g; Carbohydrate 10.9g, of which sugars 10.2g; Fat 1g, of which saturates 0.5g; Cholesterol 56mg; Calcium 104mg; Fibre 1.3g; Sodium 877mg.

Northern prawn and squash soup

As the title of the recipe suggests, this dish comes from northern Thailand.
It is quite hearty, something of a cross between a soup and a stew. The banana
flower isn't essential, but it does add a unique and authentic flavour.

1 Peel the butternut squash and cut it in half. Scoop out the seeds with a teaspoon
and discard, then cut the flesh into neat cubes. Set aside.

2 Make the chilli paste by pounding the shallots, peppercorns, chilli and shrimp paste
together using a mortar and pestle, or puréeing them in a spice blender.

3 Heat the stock gently in a large pan, then stir in the chilli paste. Add the squash,
beans and banana flower, if using. Bring to the boil and cook for 15 minutes.

4 Add the fish sauce, prawns and basil. Bring to simmering point, then simmer
for 3 minutes. Serve in warmed bowls, accompanied by rice.

Serves four

1 butternut squash, about 300g/11oz

1 litre/1¾ pints/4 cups vegetable stock

90g/3½oz/scant 1 cup green beans,
cut into 2.5cm/1in pieces

45g/1¾oz dried banana flower
(optional)

15ml/1 tbsp Thai fish sauce

225g/8oz raw prawns (shrimp)

small bunch fresh basil

cooked rice, to serve

For the chilli paste

115g/4oz shallots, sliced

10 drained bottled green peppercorns

1 small fresh green chilli, seeded and
finely chopped

2.5ml/½ tsp shrimp paste

Energy 67kcal/284kJ; Protein 11.5g; Carbohydrate 3.6g, of which sugars 2.9g; Fat 0.9g, of which saturates 0.2g; Cholesterol 110mg; Calcium 82mg; Fibre 1.7g; Sodium 409mg.

Coconut and seafood soup

The long list of ingredients for this recipe could mislead you into thinking that this soup is complicated and very time-consuming to prepare. In fact, it is extremely easy to put together, and the marriage of flavours works beautifully.

1 Pour the fish stock into a large pan and add the slices of galangal or ginger, the lemon grass and half the shredded kaffir lime leaves.

2 Reserve a few garlic chives for the garnish, then chop the remainder. Add half the chopped garlic chives to the pan. Strip the coriander leaves from the stalks and set the leaves aside. Add the stalks to the pan. Bring to the boil, reduce the heat to low and cover the pan, then simmer gently for 20 minutes. Strain the stock into a bowl.

3 Rinse and dry the pan. Add the oil and shallots. Cook over a medium heat for 5–10 minutes, until the shallots are just beginning to brown.

4 Stir in the strained stock, coconut milk, the remaining kaffir lime leaves and 30ml/2 tbsp of the fish sauce. Heat gently until simmering, and cook over a low heat for 5–10 minutes.

5 Stir in the curry paste and prawns, then cook for 3 minutes. Add the squid and cook for a further 2 minutes. Add the lime juice, if using, and season, adding more fish sauce to taste. Stir in the remaining chives and the reserved coriander leaves. Serve in bowls and sprinkle each portion with fried shallots and whole garlic chives.

Serves four

600ml/1 pint/2½ cups fish stock

5 thin slices fresh galangal or fresh root ginger

2 lemon grass stalks, chopped

3 kaffir lime leaves, shredded

bunch garlic chives, about 25g/1oz

small bunch fresh coriander (cilantro), about 15g/½oz

15ml/1 tbsp vegetable oil

4 shallots, chopped

400ml/14fl oz can coconut milk

30–45ml/2–3 tbsp Thai fish sauce

45–60ml/3–4 tbsp Thai green curry paste

450g/1lb raw large prawns (shrimp), peeled and deveined

450g/1lb prepared squid

a little fresh lime juice (optional)

salt and ground black pepper

60ml/4 tbsp crisp fried shallot slices, to serve

Energy 253kcal/1068kJ; Protein 37.8g; Carbohydrate 6.9g, of which sugars 5.5g; Fat 8.5g, of which saturates 1.6g; Cholesterol 473mg; Calcium 135mg; Fibre 0.1g; Sodium 930mg.

MALAYSIA

Steaming bowls of fragrant, clear broth brimming with noodles, vegetables, succulent seafood and tender meat are the staple fare of hawker stalls and coffee shops in Malaysia. They make sustaining lunches and late-night snacks. Years ago, itinerant hawkers used to roam the streets carrying a pole laden with two baskets: one held a stove and a cooking pot; the other held the ingredients for the soup, which could be quickly rustled up for hungry customers.

Malaysian hot and sour fish soup

Ikan asam pedas is the Malay version of the hot and sour fish soup found throughout South-east Asia. The sour notes are derived from the use of tamarind, whereas the hot flavourings come from the chilli-based *rempah*, the foundation of many Malaysian soups and curries. The Peranakans also have their own version of this hot and sour fish soup, which they serve with steamed rice. Generally, the Malays eat it with chunks of bread to dip into the highly flavoured broth.

1 To make the *rempah*, grind all the ingredients to a paste, using a mortar and pestle or food processor.

2 Heat the oil in a wok or heavy pan, and stir in the *rempah*. Fry it until it is fragrant and begins to change colour. Stir in the tamarind paste and add the snake beans, tossing them around the wok until they are coated in the spice mixture.

3 Pour in 900ml/1½ pints/3¾ cups water and bring to the boil. Reduce the heat and simmer for 5 minutes. Season with salt and pepper, then add the fish cutlets. Cook gently for 2–3 minutes until cooked through, then ladle the soup into bowls. Garnish with coriander and serve with steamed rice or chunks of fresh bread.

Serves four

30ml/2 tbsp vegetable oil

15–30ml/1–2 tbsp tamarind paste

115g/4oz snake beans (long beans), trimmed

450g/1lb fish cutlets (such as trout, cod, sea perch, pike), about 2.5cm/1in thick

fresh coriander (cilantro) leaves, to garnish

rice or bread, to serve

For the *rempah*

8 dried red chillies, soaked in warm water until soft, drained and seeded

8 shallots, chopped

4 garlic cloves, chopped

2 lemon grass stalks, trimmed and sliced

25g/1oz fresh galangal, chopped

25g/1oz fresh turmeric, chopped

5ml/1 tsp shrimp paste

Energy 164Kcal/686kJ; Protein 21.7g; Carbohydrate 4.9g, of which sugars 3.5g; Fat 6.5g, of which saturates 0.8g; Cholesterol 52mg; Calcium 33mg; Fibre 1.3g; Sodium 69mg.

Serves four to six

For the fish balls

450g/1lb fresh fish fillets (such as haddock, cod, whiting or bream), boned and flaked

15–30ml/1–2 tbsp rice flour

salt and ground black pepper

For the soup

1.5 litres/2½ pints/6¼ cups fish or chicken stock

15–30ml/1–2 tbsp light soy sauce

4–6 mustard green leaves, chopped

90g/3½oz mung bean thread noodles, soaked in hot water until soft

For the garnish

2 spring onions (scallions), trimmed and finely sliced

1 red or green chilli, seeded and finely sliced

fresh coriander (cilantro) leaves, finely chopped

Fish ball soup

This light, Chinese-inspired soup can be found in coffee shops and at the *tze char* stalls, where the food is ordered from the menu and cooked on the spot. Often eaten as a snack or light lunch, the soup is garnished with spring onions and fresh chillies, and the Malays often add an extra drizzle of chilli sauce or a dollop of chilli sambal.

1 To make the fish balls, grind the flaked flesh to a paste, using a mortar and pestle or food processor. Season with salt and pepper and stir in 60ml/4 tbsp water. Add enough rice flour to form a paste. Take small portions of fish paste into your hands and squeeze them to mould into balls.

2 Meanwhile, bring the stock to the boil in a deep pan and season to taste with soy sauce. Drop in the fish balls and simmer for 5 minutes. Add the shredded mustard greens and cook for 1 minute.

3 Divide the noodles among four to six bowls. Using a slotted spoon, add the fish balls and greens to the noodles, then ladle over the hot stock. Garnish with the spring onions and chilli, and sprinkle the chopped coriander over the top.

Cook's tip Ready-to-cook fish balls, widely available frozen in most Asian supermarkets, need only to be defrosted before adding to the dish.

Energy 127Kcal/533kJ; Protein 14.9g; Carbohydrate 14.8g, of which sugars 0.5g; Fat 0.6g, of which saturates 0.1g; Cholesterol 35mg; Calcium 17mg; Fibre 0.2g; Sodium 408mg.

Serves four

120g/4oz fresh prawns (shrimp), shelled

100g/3¾oz minced (ground) pork

5ml/1 tsp salt

5ml/1 tsp cornflour (cornstarch)

12 won ton wrappers

600ml/1 pint/2½ cups water

1 seafood stock cube

1 spring onion (scallion), trimmed and chopped, to garnish

freshly ground black pepper

Cook's tip Won ton wrappers are thin yellow pastry sheets made from egg and wheat flour. They are widely available in Asian supermarkets, and can be bought fresh or frozen.

Won ton soup

Possibly the best-travelled Chinese dish of all, won ton soup is now ubiquitous in restaurants, hawker centres and food courts throughout South-east Asia. Won tons arrived with Cantonese and Hakka migrants from South China and, in time, were adopted by the locals. This soup is one of the easiest and tastiest starters to prepare at home. Adding a little cornflour to the filling gives it a smooth texture.

1 Grind the prawns finely using a pestle and mortar or a food processor and mix with the pork, salt and cornflour.

2 Lay a won ton wrapper flat on the work surface and moisten the edges with water. Place a scant teaspoonful of the mixture in the centre and gather up the sides around the filling to make a tight ball, pressing the wrapper firmly together at the neck to leave a little frill at the top. Repeat with the remaining mixture and won ton wrappers.

3 Bring a pot of water to the boil. Drop in the won tons and cook them for 3 minutes. Drain and set aside.

4 Bring the measured water to the boil, crumble in the stock cube and stir to dissolve. Drop the cooked won tons into the hot stock and cook for 1 minute.

5 Garnish with chopped spring onions and season with black pepper. Divide among four serving bowls and serve the soup immediately.

Energy 134Kcal/568kJ; Protein 13.6g; Carbohydrate 16.3g, of which sugars 1.9g; Fat 2.1g, of which saturates 0.7g; Cholesterol 52mg; Calcium 42mg; Fibre 0.6g; Sodium 589mg.

Mooli and prawn soup

Serves four

150g/5oz mooli (daikon), peeled

700ml/1¼ pints/2¾ cups water

5ml/1 tsp salt

15ml/1 tbsp sesame oil

115g/4oz prawns (shrimp), shelled

1 spring onion (scallion), trimmed and chopped

freshly ground black pepper

This very simple soup of Cantonese origin is often drunk as a cooling brew to counteract a surfeit of spicy dishes. Mooli is full of flavour and has an important place within the range of Chinese Yin foods purported to dispel body heat.

1 Slice the peeled mooli into thin matchstick pieces. Bring water to the boil, add the mooli, salt and sesame oil and simmer for 15 minutes.

2 Add the prawns and simmer for 5 minutes.

3 Scatter with chopped spring onion, add black pepper to taste and serve immediately.

Cook's tip Mooli is the Hindi name for the large white radish or daikon. It looks rather like a parsnip, but is actually related to the radish. The flavour is milder than that of most radishes, however, although the texture is crisp and crunchy like a radish.

Energy 52kcal/215kJ; Protein 5.4g; Carbohydrate 0.8g, of which sugars 0.8g; Fat 3g, of which saturates 0.5g; Cholesterol 56mg; Calcium 31mg; Fibre 0.4g; Sodium 550mg.

Noodles in spicy tangy soup

This is a classic Nonya dish called *mee siam* (its antecedents hail from Chiang Mai, hence the name) that comes in several guises. It is really a plated dish, but street vendors sell a version that is awash in gravy, probably with regard to bottom-line profits! It is also widely available throughout Malaysia, although as a soup or dry dish it depends on who is selling it.

Serves four

vegetable oil, for deep-frying

225g/8oz firm tofu, rinsed, drained and cut into cubes

60ml/4 tbsp dried prawns (shrimp), soaked until rehydrated

5ml/1 tsp shrimp paste

4 garlic cloves, chopped

4–6 dried red chillies, soaked to soften, drained, seeded and the pulp scraped out

90g/3½oz/¾ cup roasted peanuts, ground

50g/2oz salted soya beans

2 lemon grass stalks, trimmed, halved and bruised

30ml/2 tbsp sugar

15–30ml/1–2 tbsp tamarind paste

150g/5oz dried rice vermicelli, soaked in hot water until pliable

a handful of beansprouts, rinsed and drained

4 quail's eggs, hard-boiled, shelled and halved

2 spring onions (scallions), finely sliced

salt and ground black pepper

fresh coriander (cilantro) leaves, finely chopped, to garnish

1 In a wok, heat enough vegetable oil for deep-frying. Drop in the tofu and deep-fry until golden. Drain on kitchen paper and set aside.

2 Using a mortar and pestle or food processor, grind the soaked dried prawns with the shrimp paste, garlic and chilli pulp to form a paste.

3 Heat 30ml/2 tbsp of vegetable oil in a wok and stir in the paste. Fry for 1 minute until fragrant, then add the peanuts, salted soya beans and lemon grass.

4 Fry for another minute and stir in the sugar and tamarind paste, followed by 900ml/1½ pints/3¾ cups water. Mix well and bring to the boil. Reduce the heat and simmer gently for 10 minutes. Season with salt and pepper.

5 Drain the noodles and, using a sieve (strainer) or perforated ladle, plunge the noodles into the broth to heat through. Divide the noodles among individual serving bowls, sprinkle over the beansprouts and add the deep-fried tofu, halved quail's eggs and spring onions. Ladle the spicy broth over the top, garnish with the coriander and serve immediately.

Cook's tip This is such a tasty, spicy dish that it is best served on its own as a light meal or nourishing snack, so that the flavours can be fully appreciated.

Energy 547Kcal/2280kJ; Protein 29.5g; Carbohydrate 42.5g, of which sugars 10g; Fat 29g, of which saturates 4.4g; Cholesterol 48mg; Calcium 389mg; Fibre 3.7g; Sodium 203mg.

SINGAPORE

As the melting pot of many cultures and traditions, Singapore has earned a reputation for serving some of the best global cuisines. Known as much for sophisticated fine dining as for scrumptious hawker fare, her dishes have become iconic. Most locals enjoy a wide range of soupy dishes that hail from somewhere else but are resolutely Singaporean in nature. Millions of Singaporeans have been weaned on Hokkien Prawn Noodle Soup and luscious Singapore Laksa, both deserving of the culinary hall of fame.

Spicy chicken soup

This fragrant soup, *soto ayam*, is particularly popular in Singapore. Originally from Java, various versions are served at soup and noodle stalls specializing in Indonesian and Malay food. As many Malay Singaporeans came from Indonesia, it is always in demand. When served as a meal on its own, deep-fried potato fritters or chips (French fries) or the Malay compressed rice cakes, *ketupat*, are added to the soup.

1 Using a mortar and pestle or a food processor, grind all the *rempah* ingredients to a paste. Set aside.

2 Put the chicken, lemon grass, ginger, lime leaves and chilli into a deep pan and pour in enough water to just cover. Bring to the boil, reduce the heat, cover and simmer for about 1 hour, until the chicken is tender. Remove the chicken from the stock, take off and discard the skin and tear the meat into shreds. Strain the stock.

3 In a wok or heavy pan, heat the oil. Stir in the *rempah* and cook for 1–2 minutes, until fragrant. Pour in the stock and stir well. Season to taste with salt and pepper.

4 Divide the noodles among six bowls. Add the hard-boiled eggs, beansprouts and shredded chicken. Ladle the steaming broth into each bowl and garnish with coriander. Serve immediately with the lime wedges, chilli oil and soy sauce to squeeze, drizzle and pour over it.

Serves six

1 small chicken, about 900g/2lb

2 lemon grass stalks, bruised

25g/1oz fresh root ginger, peeled and sliced

2 fresh kaffir lime leaves

1 dried red chilli

30ml/2 tbsp vegetable oil

50g/2oz mung bean thread noodles, soaked until pliable

3 hard-boiled eggs, peeled and halved

115g/4oz beansprouts

a small bunch of fresh coriander (cilantro), roughly chopped, to garnish

2 limes, quartered, chilli oil and soy sauce, to serve

For the *rempah*

8 shallots, chopped

8 garlic cloves, chopped

6 candlenuts or macadamia nuts

50g/2oz galangal, chopped

2 lemon grass stalks, chopped

4 fresh kaffir lime leaves

15ml/1 tbsp ground coriander

10ml/2 tsp ground turmeric

15ml/1 tbsp vegetable oil

Energy 493Kcal/2050kJ; Protein 36g; Carbohydrate 8.5g, of which sugars 1g; Fat 35.1g, of which saturates 9.1g; Cholesterol 258mg; Calcium 47mg; Fibre 0.8g; Sodium 178mg.

Serves four to six

1 chicken, about 1kg/2¼lb

2 chicken feet (optional)

2 cinnamon sticks

5ml/1 tsp black peppercorns

5ml/1 tsp fennel seeds

5ml/1 tsp cumin seeds

15 ml/1 tbsp ghee or vegetable oil with a little butter

15–30ml/1–2 tbsp brown mustard seeds

a handful of fresh curry leaves

salt and ground black pepper

2 limes, quartered, to serve

For the curry paste

40g/1½oz fresh root ginger, peeled and chopped

4 garlic cloves, chopped

4 shallots, chopped

2 lemon grass stalks, trimmed and chopped

4 dried red chillies, soaked to soften, drained, seeded and the pulp scraped out

15–30ml/1–2 tbsp Indian curry powder

Eurasian curried soup

With a culinary culture born from Indian, Malay, Chinese and European traditions, the Eurasians have some distinct dishes of their own. As they trace their roots to Malacca during the Portuguese and Dutch periods, many of the dishes are linked to that region and employ Portuguese methods, such as cooking in earthenware pots. In this recipe, chicken feet are sometimes added to the stock to enrich it, but these are optional.

1 To make the curry paste, grind the ginger with the garlic, shallots and lemon grass, using a mortar and pestle or food processor. Add the chilli pulp and curry powder and set aside.

2 Put the chicken and the chicken feet, if using, in a deep pan with the cinnamon sticks, peppercorns, fennel and cumin seeds. Add enough water to just cover, and bring it to the boil. Reduce the heat and cook gently for about 1 hour, until the chicken is cooked. Remove the chicken from the broth, skin it and shred the meat. Strain the broth.

3 In an earthenware pot or wok, heat the ghee or oil. Stir in the mustard seeds and, once they begin to pop and give off a nutty aroma, add the curry paste. Fry the paste until fragrant, then pour in the strained broth. Bring the broth to the boil and season to taste with salt and pepper. Add the curry leaves and shredded chicken, and ladle the soup into bowls. Serve with wedges of lime to squeeze into the soup.

Energy 264Kcal/1093kJ; Protein 20.7g; Carbohydrate 1.6g, of which sugars 1g; Fat 19.4g, of which saturates 6.3g; Cholesterol 112mg; Calcium 19mg; Fibre 0.5g; Sodium 104mg.

Serves four to six

500g/1¼lb meaty pork ribs, trimmed and cut into 5cm/2in lengths

225g/8oz pork loin

8 garlic cloves, unpeeled and bruised

2 cinnamon sticks

5 star anise

120ml/4fl oz/½ cup light soy sauce

50ml/2fl oz/¼ cup dark soy sauce

15ml/1 tbsp sugar

salt and ground black pepper

steamed rice, to serve

For the dipping sauce

120ml/4fl oz/½ cup light soy sauce

2 red chillies, seeded and finely chopped

For the spice bag

6 cloves

15ml/1 tbsp dried orange peel

5ml/1 tsp black peppercorns

5ml/1 tsp coriander seeds

5ml/1 tsp fennel seeds

a piece of muslin (cheesecloth)

Pork bone tea

The literal translation of *bak kut teh* as pork bone tea doesn't do enough justice to this aromatic, peppery broth made from pork ribs and sometimes the internal organs of the pig. It is a favourite at late-night hawker stalls and coffee shops, where it is particularly popular with the older folk, who sip it when they gather for a chat. The broth is served with bowls of steamed white rice, and the tender pork flesh is dipped into soy sauce infused with chillies.

1 To make the dipping sauce, stir the soy sauce and chillies together in a small bowl and set aside. To make the spice bag, lay the piece of muslin flat and place all the spices in the centre. Gather up the edges and tie together to form a bag.

2 Put the pork ribs and loin into a deep pan. Add the garlic, cinnamon sticks, star anise and spice bag. Pour in 2.5 litres/4½ pints/10 cups water and bring to the boil.

3 Skim off any fat from the surface, then stir in the soy sauces and sugar. Reduce the heat and simmer, partially covered, for about 2 hours, until the pork is almost falling off the bones. Season to taste with salt and lots of black pepper.

4 Remove the loin from the broth and cut it into bitesize pieces. Divide the meat and ribs among four to six bowls and ladle the steaming broth over the top. Serve with the soy and chilli sauce as a dip for the pieces of pork, and steamed rice.

Energy 49Kcal/206kJ; Protein 8.1g; Carbohydrate 0.8g, of which sugars 0.8g; Fat 1.5g, of which saturates 0.5g; Cholesterol 24mg; Calcium 3mg; Fibre 0g; Sodium 145mg.

Hokkien prawn noodle soup

Introduced to Malaysia and Singapore by the Chinese from Fujian, this soup – known as *hay mee* – is sold at hawker stalls and in coffee shops. Since most of the Chinese population of Singapore is Hokkien, it is a very popular dish. Traditionally, prawn noodle soup is served with crispy cubes of pork fat, but in this recipe crispy bacon is used instead.

1 Put all the stock ingredients into a deep pan along with the prawn shells. Pour in 2 litres/3½ pints/7¾ cups water and bring to the boil. Reduce the heat and simmer gently, uncovered, for about 2 hours, until the stock has reduced by half.

2 Strain the stock into a clean pan and put it over a low heat to keep hot. Season with salt and pepper to taste.

3 In a small pan, heat the sugar with 15ml/1 tbsp water, until it turns a rich brown. Add it to the stock and mix well. In a heavy pan, dry-fry the bacon until it turns crispy and golden. Drain on kitchen paper and set aside.

4 Using a perforated ladle or sieve (strainer), plunge the noodles into the hot stock for 1 minute to heat through, then divide them among four bowls. Add the prawns to the stock, heat for 1 minute, remove with a slotted spoon and add to the bowls. Add the beansprouts to the prawns and noodles and ladle the hot stock into the bowls. Scatter the crispy bacon and spring onions over the top and serve immediately.

Serves four to six

For the stock

45ml/3 tbsp dried shrimp

1 dried red chilli

50g/2oz fresh root ginger, peeled and sliced

2 onions, quartered

4 cloves garlic, bruised

2 lemon grass stalks, bruised

2.5ml/½ tsp black peppercorns

30–45ml/2–3 tbsp dark soy sauce

700g/1lb 10oz pork and chicken bones

For the soup

15ml/1 tbsp sugar

6 rashers (strips) streaky (fatty) bacon, sliced

150g/5oz fresh egg noodles

20 fresh, large prawns (shrimp), peeled (add the shells to the stock)

90g/3½oz beansprouts

2 spring onions (scallions), trimmed and finely sliced

salt and ground black pepper

Energy 257Kcal/1082kJ; Protein 18.7g; Carbohydrate 27.1g, of which sugars 6.9g; Fat 9g, of which saturates 2.8g; Cholesterol 94mg; Calcium 145mg; Fibre 3g; Sodium 1080mg.

Singapore laksa

There are as many laksa dishes as there are diverse regions in Malaysia and Singapore. The basic dish consists of noodles in a spicy coconut broth. In the home-cooked Singapore laksa, slices of deep-fried fish cakes are often added at the end, whereas the stall version is rich in a variety of seafood, topped with cockles.

1 Using a mortar and pestle or food processor, grind all the ingredients for the spice paste mixture, apart from the oil. Bind the paste with the oil and set aside.

2 Heat enough oil in a wok to deep-fry. Add the shallots to the oil and deep-fry until crispy and golden. Drain and set aside.

3 Heat 30ml/2 tbsp vegetable oil in a large wok or heavy pan. Stir in the spice paste and cook over a low heat for 3–4 minutes, until fragrant. Add the coconut milk and chicken stock and bring to the boil, stirring all the time. Add the prawns, squid and scallops and simmer gently, for about 5–10 minutes, until cooked. Add the cockles at the last minute, and season the broth with salt and pepper.

4 Ladle the noodles into individual bowls. Add the beansprouts and ladle over the broth and seafood, making sure the noodles are submerged in the steaming liquid. Garnish with the crispy shallots, mint and a drizzle of chilli oil.

Serves four to six

For the spice paste

8 shallots, chopped

4 garlic cloves, chopped

40g/1½oz fresh root ginger, peeled and chopped

2 lemon grass stalks, chopped

6 candlenuts or macadamia nuts

4 dried red chillies, soaked until soft, and seeded

30ml/2 tbsp dried prawns (shrimp), soaked until soft

5–10ml/1–2 tsp belacan

5–10ml/1–2 tsp sugar

15ml/1 tbsp vegetable oil

For the laksa

vegetable oil, for deep-frying

6 shallots, finely sliced

600ml/1 pint/2½ cups coconut milk

400ml/14fl oz/1⅔ cups chicken stock

90g/3½oz prawns (shrimp), shelled

90g/3½oz squid, cleaned, trimmed and sliced

6–8 scallops

75g/3oz cockles, shelled

225g/8oz fresh rice noodles or dried rice vermicelli, soaked in lukewarm water until pliable

90g/3½oz beansprouts

salt and ground black pepper

a small bunch of Vietnamese mint or fresh garden mint, roughly chopped, and chilli oil, to garnish

Energy 300Kcal/1254kJ; Protein 14.2g; Carbohydrate 38g, of which sugars 6.9g; Fat 10.3g, of which saturates 1.4g; Cholesterol 77mg; Calcium 69mg; Fibre 0.7g; Sodium 211mg.

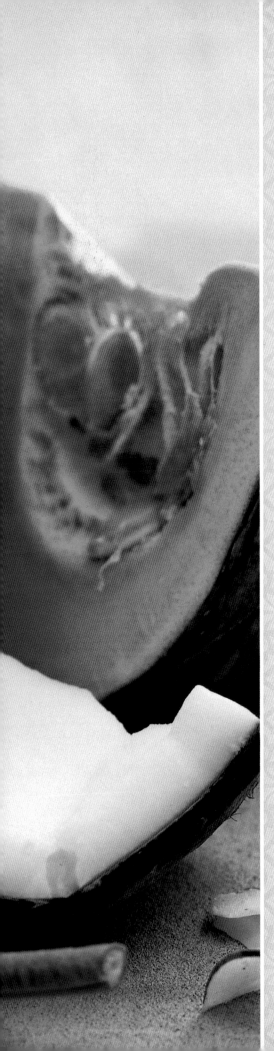

INDONESIA

Many dishes featured here are meals in themselves – satisfying, warming bowls of meat, seafood and vegetables, bathed in spicy, fragrant broth. If you are serving one of these dishes as an appetizer, small portions with colourful garnishes are ideal; if the soup is the main feature of the meal, then ladle plenty into each bowl and enjoy it with crusty bread or a side dish of rice to soak up the flavours.

Unripe papaya soup

This is a lightly spiced and herby soup from Indonesia that makes good use of unripe papaya, and is an ideal start to any meal. It is the kind of soup meant to prepare the tastebuds for what is yet to come – light and refreshing to the palate.

Serves four

1 unripe papaya, about 800g/1¾lb

45ml/3 tbsp vegetable oil

1 litre/1¾ pints/4 cups water

4 salam leaves (Indonesian bay leaves) or sweet basil leaves

2 lemon grass stalks, 5cm/2in of root end bruised

2.5ml/½ tsp ground black pepper

5ml/1 tsp salt

fried shallots or serundeng, to garnish

For the spice paste

2 lemon grass stalks, 5cm/2in of root end finely chopped

6 shallots, finely chopped

5 garlic cloves, finely chopped

10g/¼oz galangal

15g/½oz terasi (Indonesian shrimp paste)

2.5ml/½ tsp turmeric powder

4 fresh red chillies, seeded and finely chopped

5ml/1 tsp coriander seeds

10g/¼oz *kencur* root (lesser galangal)

1 Grind the spice paste ingredients to a textured paste using a pestle and mortar or an electric food processor or blender.

2 Peel the papaya with a vegetable peeler and slice into two lengthways. Discard any soft pulp and seeds. Slice the papaya into long strips and then crossways into pieces about 5mm/¼in thick.

3 Heat the oil and fry the spice paste over a low heat for 10 minutes, stirring constantly until the fragrances are released and the oil separates.

4 Bring the water to the boil and stir in the fried spice paste. Simmer for 3 minutes. Add the papaya slices, salam leaves, lemon grass, pepper and salt. Cook for 5–8 minutes until the papaya slices are just tender.

5 While the papaya is cooking, prepare your garnishes of fried sliced shallots or serundeng and warm the soup bowls.

6 Take the papaya soup off the heat. Adjust the seasoning if necessary and serve it in individual bowls, garnished as you wish.

Cook's tip It can be difficult to find salam leaves outside of large Asian markets, but fresh bay leaves will work in this recipe and may be used instead.

Energy 189kcal/791kJ; Protein 5.1g; Carbohydrate 21.8g, of which sugars 18.8g; Fat 9.8g, of which saturates 1.1g; Cholesterol 19mg; Calcium 137mg; Fibre 5.2g; Sodium 181mg.

Pumpkin, snake bean and bamboo soup with coconut

This tasty soup is from Java, where it is served on its own with rice or as an accompaniment to a poached or grilled fish dish. In some parts of Java, the dish includes small prawns but, if it is packed with vegetables alone, it makes an extremely satisfying vegetarian meal. Generally, *sayur* dishes are accompanied by a chilli sambal, which can be made by pounding chillies with shrimp paste and lime juice, or with ginger and garlic.

1 To make the spice paste, using a mortar and pestle, grind all the ingredients together to form a smooth paste, or whiz them together in an electric blender or food processor.

2 Heat the oil in a wok or large, heavy pan, stir in the spice paste and fry until fragrant. Toss the pumpkin, snake beans and bamboo shoots in the paste and pour in the coconut milk. Add the sugar and bring to the boil. Reduce the heat and cook gently for 5–10 minutes, until the vegetables are tender.

3 Season the soup with salt to taste, and stir in half the fresh coconut. Ladle the soup into individual warmed bowls, sprinkle with the remaining coconut and serve with bowls of cooked rice to spoon the soup over and a chilli sambal.

Cook's tip Bamboo shoots are available in cans in most Chinese and South-east Asian markets and stores and large supermarkets.

Variation When pumpkins are not in season, you could use a different member of the squash family, such as butternut squash or acorn squash.

Serves four

30ml/2 tbsp palm, groundnut (peanut) or corn oil

150g/5oz pumpkin flesh

115g/4oz snake beans (yardlong beans)

220g/7½oz can bamboo shoots, drained and rinsed

900ml/1½ pints coconut milk

10–15ml/2–3 tsp palm sugar

130g/4½oz fresh coconut, shredded

salt

For the spice paste

4 shallots, chopped

25g/1oz fresh root ginger, chopped

4 red chillies, seeded and chopped

2 garlic cloves, chopped

5ml/1 tsp coriander seeds

4 candlenuts, toasted and chopped

To serve

cooked rice

chilli sambal

Energy 333kcal/1388kJ; Protein 6g; Carbohydrate 26g, of which sugars 23.8g; Fat 23.6g, of which saturates 11.7g; Cholesterol 0mg; Calcium 115mg; Fibre 4.9g; Sodium 258mg.

Indonesian chicken broth

This is perhaps the most popular of all Indonesian soups. Throughout South-east Asia you will find variations of this soup; even in Indonesia it varies from region to region, such as the Bali version that includes noodles instead of potatoes. Colourful and crunchy, this classic soup can be served as an appetizer or as a light and refreshing dish on its own.

1 First prepare the ingredients for serving by putting the coriander, spring onions, chillies and lime wedges into a serving bowl.

2 Heat the oil in a heavy pan, stir in the ginger, turmeric, lemon grass, kaffir lime leaves, candlenuts, garlic, coriander seeds and terasi and fry until the mixture begins to darken and become fragrant. Pour in the chicken stock, bring to the boil, then reduce the heat and simmer for about 20 minutes.

3 Meanwhile, heat the oil for deep-frying in a wok. Add the potato slices and fry until crisp and golden brown. Remove from the pan with a slotted spoon, drain on kitchen paper and put aside.

4 Strain the flavoured chicken stock and reserve. Pour back into the pan and season with salt and pepper to taste. Return to the boil, then reduce the heat and add the chicken. Simmer for 2–3 minutes until cooked but still tender.

5 Quickly prepare four to six soup bowls by sprinkling some of the cabbage and mung bean sprouts into the base of each. Ladle the broth over the cabbage and bean sprouts, dividing the chicken equally between the bowls, and arrange the sliced boiled eggs and deep-fried potatoes over the top.

6 Serve the hot broth with the ingredients for serving, so that each diner can add them to their own bowls, and pass around the *kecap manis* to drizzle over the top.

Variation Instead of waxy potatoes, you could try using finely sliced sweet potato, yam or plantain.

Serves four to six

30ml/2 tbsp palm, groundnut (peanut) or corn oil

25g/1oz fresh root ginger, finely chopped

25g/1oz fresh turmeric, finely chopped, or 5ml/1 tsp ground turmeric

1 lemon grass stalk, finely chopped

4–5 kaffir lime leaves, crushed with fingers

4 candlenuts, coarsely ground

2 garlic cloves, crushed

5ml/1 tsp coriander seeds

5ml/1 tsp terasi (Indonesian shrimp paste)

2 litres/3½ pints/8 cups chicken stock

corn or vegetable oil, for deep-frying

2 waxy potatoes, finely sliced

350g/12oz skinless chicken breast fillets, thinly sliced widthways

150g/5oz leafy green cabbage, finely sliced

150g/5oz mung bean sprouts

3 hard-boiled eggs, thinly sliced

salt and ground black pepper

To serve

1 bunch fresh coriander (cilantro) leaves, roughly chopped

2–3 spring onions (scallions), finely sliced

2–3 hot red or green chillies, seeded and finely sliced diagonally

2 limes, cut into wedges

kecap manis (Indonesian sweet soy sauce)

Energy 296kcal/1238kJ; Protein 21.1g; Carbohydrate 14.8g, of which sugars 3g; Fat 17.5g, of which saturates 2.8g; Cholesterol 136mg; Calcium 63mg; Fibre 2.7g; Sodium 96mg.

Spicy aubergine soup with beef and lime

A delicious soupy stew from North Sumatra, this soup can be made with aubergines, green jackfruit or any of the squash family. For an authentic meal, serve the dish with a bowl of rice and a chilli sambal, bearing in mind that the quantity of rice should be greater than the soupy stew, as the role of the soup is to moisten and flavour the rice.

1 To make the spice paste, using a mortar and pestle, grind all the ingredients together to form a textured paste, or whiz them together in an electric blender or food processor.

2 Heat the oil in a wok or heavy pan, stir in the spice paste and fry until fragrant. Add the beef, stirring to coat it well in the spice paste, then add the coconut milk and sugar. Bring the liquid to the boil, then reduce the heat and simmer gently for 10 minutes.

3 Add the aubergine wedges and kaffir lime leaves to the pan and cook gently for a further 5–10 minutes, until tender but not mushy. Stir in the lime juice and season with salt to taste.

4 Ladle the soup into individual warmed bowls and serve with bowls of cooked rice to spoon the soup over, wedges of lime to squeeze on the top and a chilli sambal.

Cook's tip Since there are a variety of aubergines (eggplants) available in different parts of the world, and they come in many different shapes and sizes, use your judgement about how much you need, and ensure the flesh is cut into bitesize chunks.

Serves four

30ml/2 tbsp palm, groundnut (peanut) or corn oil

150g/5oz lean beef, cut into thin strips

500ml/17fl oz/generous 2 cups coconut milk

10ml/2 tsp sugar

3–4 Thai aubergines (eggplants) or 1 large Mediterranean aubergine, cut into wedges

3–4 kaffir lime leaves

juice of 1 lime

salt

For the spice paste

4 shallots, chopped

4 red Thai chillies, seeded and chopped

25g/1oz fresh root ginger, chopped

15g/½oz fresh turmeric, chopped or 2.5ml/½ tsp ground turmeric

2 garlic cloves, chopped

5ml/1 tsp coriander seeds

2.5ml/½ tsp cumin seeds

2–3 candlenuts

To serve

cooked rice

1 lime, quartered

chilli sambal

Energy 224kcal/938kJ; Protein 12.1g; Carbohydrate 14.6g, of which sugars 12.6g; Fat 13.6g, of which saturates 3.2g; Cholesterol 22mg; Calcium 79mg; Fibre 3g; Sodium 181mg.

Spicy tripe soup with lemon grass and lime

This popular Indonesian soup is packed with spices and the refreshing flavours of lemon grass and lime. Steaming bowls of *soto babat* are sought after at food stalls as a great pick-me-up. The locals prefer their tripe to be chewy for this spicy soup, which is served with a pungent chilli sambal, but if you prefer, you can cook it for longer so that the tripe is tender.

1 Fill a large pan with about 2.5 litres/4½ pints/11¼ cups water and bring it to the boil. Reduce the heat and stir in the vinegar. Add the tripe, season with salt and pepper and simmer gently for about 1 hour.

2 Meanwhile, prepare the sambal. Heat the oil in a small, heavy pan. Stir in the garlic and chillies and fry until fragrant. Stir in the chilli and shrimp paste, then add the tomato paste and mix until thoroughly combined. Tip the paste into a small dish and put aside.

3 When the tripe is cooked, drain and cut into bitesize squares or strips. Pour the stock or water into a large pan and bring it to the boil. Reduce the heat and add the tripe, garlic, lemon grass, ginger, lime leaves and mooli or turnip. Cook gently for 15–20 minutes, until the mooli or turnip is tender. (For tender tripe, omit the mooli or turnip at this stage, simmer the tripe for 4–5 hours and then add the mooli or turnip for the last 15 minutes of cooking).

4 Meanwhile, heat the oil in a small frying pan. Add the shallots and fry for about 5 minutes until golden brown. Drain on kitchen paper.

5 Ladle the soup into individual warmed bowls and sprinkle the shallots over the top. Serve the soup with the spicy sambal, which can be added in a dollop and stirred in.

Cook's tip If you prefer your tripe tender, cook it for 4–5 hours and increase the quantity of stock.

Serves four

250ml/8fl oz/1 cup rice wine vinegar

900g/2lb beef tripe, cleaned

2 litres/3½ pints/8 cups beef stock or water

2–3 garlic cloves, crushed whole

2 lemon grass stalks

25g/1oz fresh root ginger, finely grated

3–4 kaffir lime leaves

225g/8oz mooli (daikon) or turnip, finely sliced

15ml/1 tbsp palm, groundnut (peanut) or vegetable oil

4 shallots, finely sliced

salt and ground black pepper

For the sambal

15ml/1 tbsp palm, groundnut (peanut) or vegetable oil

2 garlic cloves, crushed

2–3 hot red chillies, seeded and finely chopped

15ml/1 tbsp chilli and shrimp paste

25ml/1½ tbsp tomato paste

Energy 160kcal/668kJ; Protein 19.2g; Carbohydrate 5.5g, of which sugars 4.8g; Fat 7g, of which saturates 1.1g; Cholesterol 163mg; Calcium 198mg; Fibre 1.9g; Sodium 299mg.

THE PHILIPPINES

With a long history of colonization by China, America, Spain and Japan, the cuisine of the Philippines has drawn inexhaustibly from these countries. It is Spain that has had the most impact, as the archipelago is predominantly Catholic. Chinese and Malay influences are not diffident, with noodles and spicy dishes within the menu. In Luzon especially, where there is a large Muslim community, the cooking is similar to that of Indonesia and Malaysia.

Chicken soup with coconut

Serves four

30ml/2 tbsp vegetable oil

4 garlic cloves, crushed

6 shallots, chopped

30g/1oz young fresh ginger root, grated

350g/12oz boneless chicken, diced

1 litre/1¾ pints/4 cups water

2 lemon grass stalks, 5cm/2in of root end bruised

5ml/1 tsp salt

2.5ml/½ tsp ground black pepper

1 chicken stock cube

1 young coconut, flesh grated and coconut water reserved

holy basil or coriander (cilantro) leaves, to garnish

Coconuts are grown just about everywhere in the Philippines, but it is in the southern provinces, especially Mindanao, that production is carried out on a large scale. Coconut milk as a soup base has its early beginnings in India centuries ago, but moved to the Indo-Chinese countries and then to Indonesia, the Philippines and Malaysia.

1 Heat the oil in a large frying pan or wok and fry the garlic until fragrant and golden brown. Add the shallots and grated ginger and fry for 2 minutes.

2 Add the chicken to the pan and stir-fry for 5 minutes until the pieces are white all over. Transfer to a larger pan if necessary for the next step.

3 Add the water, lemon grass, salt and pepper and crumble in the stock cube. Simmer for 25 minutes until the chicken is very tender. Add the grated coconut flesh and water and simmer for another 5 minutes. Serve garnished with fresh basil or coriander leaves.

Cook's tip The water inside a coconut is not coconut milk. Coconut milk actually comes from grating and squeezing coconut meat with a little water.

Energy 87kcal/371kJ; Protein 13.1g; Carbohydrate 6.8g, of which sugars 6.7g; Fat 1.1g, of which saturates 0.4g; Cholesterol 35mg; Calcium 42mg; Fibre 0.3g; Sodium 620mg.

Chicken and ginger broth with papaya

Serves four to six

15–30ml/1–2 tbsp palm or groundnut (peanut) oil

2 garlic cloves, finely chopped

1 large onion, sliced

40g/1½oz fresh root ginger, finely grated

2 whole dried chillies

1 chicken, left whole or jointed, trimmed of fat

30ml/2 tbsp *patis* (fish sauce)

600ml/1 pint/2½ cups chicken stock

1.2 litres/2 pints/5 cups water

1 small green papaya, cut into fine slices or strips

1 bunch fresh young chilli or basil leaves

salt and ground black pepper

cooked rice, to serve

In the Philippines, this is a traditional peasant dish that is still cooked every day in rural areas. In the province of Iloilo, located in the Western Visayas, green papaya is added to the broth, which could be regarded as a Filipino version of *coq au vin*. Generally the chicken and broth are served with steamed rice, but the broth is also sipped during the meal to cleanse and stimulate the palate.

1 Heat the oil in a wok or a large pan that has a lid. Stir in the garlic, onion and ginger and fry until they begin to colour. Stir in the chillies, add the chicken and fry until the skin is lightly browned all over.

2 Pour in the *patis*, stock and water, adding more water if necessary so that the chicken is completely covered. Bring to the boil, reduce the heat, cover and simmer gently for about 1½ hours, until the chicken is very tender.

3 Season the stock with salt and pepper and add the papaya. Continue to simmer for a further 10–15 minutes, then stir in the chilli or basil leaves. Serve the chicken and broth in warmed bowls, with bowls of steamed rice to ladle the broth over the top.

Energy 290kcal/1219kJ; Protein 46.4g; Carbohydrate 9.8g, of which sugars 8.7g; Fat 7.5g, of which saturates 1.5g; Cholesterol 169mg; Calcium 40mg; Fibre 2.2g; Sodium 150mg.

Tamarind pork and vegetable soup

Sour soups, usually flavoured with tamarind or lime, are very popular in South-east Asia. In the Philippines, the national sour soup is *sinigang*, which varies from region to region, such as the Bicolano version made with coconut milk and chillies. However, it can be made with any combination of meat or fish and vegetables, as long as it is sour. Tamarind pods or *kamias*, a sour fruit similar in shape to star fruit, are the common souring agents, as most Filipinos grow them in their gardens.

1 In a wok or deep pan, bring the stock to the boil. Stir in the tamarind paste, *patis* and ginger, reduce the heat and simmer for about 20 minutes. Season the mixture with salt and lots of pepper.

2 Add the yam and snake beans to the pan and cook gently for 3–4 minutes, until the yam is tender. Stir in the spinach and the sliced pork and simmer gently for 2–3 minutes, until the pork is just cooked and turns opaque.

3 Ladle the soup into individual warmed bowls and sprinkle the sliced spring onions over the top.

Serves four to six

2 litres/3½ pints/8 cups pork or chicken stock, or a mixture of stock and water

15–30ml/1–2 tbsp tamarind paste

30ml/2 tbsp *patis* (fish sauce)

25g/1oz fresh root ginger, finely grated

1 medium yam or sweet potato, cut into bitesize chunks

8–10 snake beans (yardlong beans)

225g/8oz kangkong (water spinach) or ordinary spinach, well rinsed

350g/12oz pork tenderloin, sliced widthways

2–3 spring onions (scallions), white parts only, finely sliced

salt and ground black pepper

Energy 126kcal/532kJ; Protein 14g; Carbohydrate 12.3g, of which sugars 4.1g; Fat 2.7g, of which saturates 0.9g; Cholesterol 37mg; Calcium 31mg; Fibre 2g; Sodium 417mg.

Serves four to six

15–30ml/1–2 tbsp palm or groundnut (peanut) oil

1 large onion, finely chopped.

2 garlic cloves, finely chopped

25g/1oz fresh root ginger, finely chopped

350g/12oz pork rump or tenderloin, cut widthways into bitesize slices

5–6 black peppercorns

115g/4oz/1 cup plus 15ml/1 tbsp short grain rice

2 litres/3½ pints/8 cups pork or chicken stock

30ml/2 tbsp *patis* (fish sauce)

salt

To serve

2 garlic cloves, finely chopped

2 spring onions (scallions), white parts only, finely sliced

2–3 green or red chillies, seeded and quartered lengthways

Colonial rice soup with pork and roasted garlic

Made with pork or chicken, this warming and sustaining rice soup combines the ancient traditions of the Filipino rice culture with the Spanish colonial culinary techniques of browning and sautéing.

1 Heat the oil in a wok or deep, heavy pan that has a lid. Stir in the onion, garlic and ginger and fry until fragrant and beginning to colour. Add the pork and then fry, stirring frequently, for 5–6 minutes, until lightly browned. Stir in the peppercorns.

2 Meanwhile, put the rice in a sieve (strainer), rinse under cold running water until the water runs clear, then drain. Toss the rice into the pan, making sure that it is coated in the mixture. Pour in the stock, add the *patis* and bring to the boil. Reduce the heat and partially cover with a lid. Simmer for about 40 minutes, stirring ocassionally to make sure that the rice doesn't stick to the bottom of the pan. Season with salt to taste.

3 Just before serving, dry-fry the garlic in a small, heavy pan, until golden brown, then stir it into the soup. Ladle the soup into individual warmed bowls and sprinkle the spring onions over the top. Serve the chillies separately, to chew on.

Energy 195kcal/813kJ; Protein 14.8g; Carbohydrate 19.9g, of which sugars 3.4g; Fat 6.2g, of which saturates 1.3g; Cholesterol 37mg; Calcium 24mg; Fibre 0.8g; Sodium 399mg.

Beef and heart of palm soup

Filipino beef soups can range from the very subtle and light to hearty concoctions that are practically stews. This one, using hearts of palm, sits somewhere in between, with its clear but highly flavoured stock. It tastes even better if you use bones to make the stock (see Cook's tip). Traditionalists would use banana plant hearts, but these can be hard to find. Hearts of palm are readily available in cans from supermarkets.

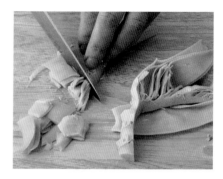

1 Slice the beef, then cut it into cubes no larger than 2cm/¾in.

2 Put the beef into a pan with the water and onion, bring to the boil, then simmer for 1½ hours uncovered, to reduce the stock by a third.

3 While the stock is simmering, slice the palm hearts.

4 Add the sliced hearts of palm to the hot beef and onion stock and return to simmering point.

5 Add the *patis* and pepper, and simmer for 30 minutes. Serve the soup hot, garnished with the shallots or garlic.

Serves four

800g/1¾lb beef brisket or shank

1.5 litres/2⅔ pints/6 cups water

1 large onion, finely sliced

2 hearts of palms (about 225g/8oz)

30ml/2 tbsp *patis* (Filipino fish sauce)

2.5ml/½ tsp ground black pepper

fried shallots or garlic, to garnish

Cook's tip If you can find beef bones, boil 2kg/4½lb of these in the measured water and strain, discarding the bones. Use this in place of the plain water in step 2.

Energy 384kcal/1581kJ; Protein 10g; Carbohydrate 0.7g, of which sugars 0.7g; Fat 37.4g, of which saturates 10.2g; Cholesterol 0mg; Calcium 11mg; Fibre 0g; Sodium 232mg.

Serves four to six

2 litres/3½ pints/8 cups fish stock

250ml/8fl oz/1 cup white wine

15–30ml/1–2 tbsp tamarind paste

30–45ml/2–3 tbsp *patis* (fish sauce)

30ml/2 tbsp palm sugar

50g/2oz fresh root ginger, grated

2–3 red or green chillies, seeded and finely sliced

2 tomatoes, skinned, seeded and cut into wedges

350g/12oz fresh fish, such as trout, sea bass, swordfish or cod, cut into bitesize chunks

12–16 fresh prawns (shrimp), in their shells

1 bunch fresh basil leaves, roughly chopped

1 bunch flat leaf parsley, roughly chopped

salt and ground black pepper

To serve

60–90ml/4–6 tbsp coconut vinegar

1–2 garlic cloves, finely chopped

1–2 limes, cut into wedges

2 red or green chillies, seeded and quartered lengthways

Cook's tip You can shell the prawns (shrimp) if you would prefer to, but the shells add to the flavour of the soup.

Hot and sour Filipino fish soup

Chunky, filling and satisfying, the Filipino fish soups are meals in themselves. There are many variations on the theme, depending on the region and the local fish, but most are packed with shellfish, flavoured with sour tamarind combined with hot chilli, and served with coconut vinegar flavoured with garlic. Served on its own or with rice, this soup certainly awakens the senses!

1 In a wok or large pan, bring the stock and wine to the boil. Stir in the tamarind paste, *patis*, sugar, ginger and chillies. Reduce the heat and simmer for 15–20 minutes.

2 Add the tomatoes to the broth and season with salt and pepper. Add the fish and prawns and simmer for a further 5 minutes, until the fish is cooked.

3 Meanwhile, in a bowl, quickly mix together the coconut vinegar and garlic for serving and put aside.

4 Stir half the basil and half the parsley into the broth and ladle into individual warmed bowls. Garnish with the remaining basil and parsley and serve immediately, with the spiked coconut vinegar to splash on top, the lime wedges to squeeze into the soup, and the chillies to chew on for extra heat.

Energy 137kcal/576kJ; Protein 17.7g; Carbohydrate 8.1g, of which sugars 8g; Fat 1g, of which saturates 0.1g; Cholesterol 92mg; Calcium 76mg; Fibre 1.3g; Sodium 644mg.

VIETNAM

In Vietnam, soups and broths are served for breakfast and as snacks throughout the day, as an appetizer to a meal, as accompaniments to steamed rice, and as palate cleansers between courses. At home, you may want to serve one of the more substantial soups, such as Duck and Nut Soup with Chinese Red Dates or Hot-and-Sour Fish Soup, as a meal in itself with chunks of fresh bread. Light broths, such as Pork and Lotus Root Broth, make refreshing first courses.

Tofu soup with mushrooms, tomato, ginger and coriander

This is a typical *canh* – a clear broth from the north of Vietnam. It should be light, to balance a meal that may include some heavier meat or poultry dishes. Because the soup is reliant on a well-flavoured, aromatic broth, the basic stock needs to be rich in taste.

1 To make the stock, put the chicken carcass or pork ribs in a deep pan. Drain and rinse the dried squid or shrimp. Add to the pan with the remaining stock ingredients, except the salt, and pour in 2 litres/3½ pints/8 cups water. Bring to the boil, and boil for a few minutes, skim off any foam, then reduce the heat and simmer with the lid on for 1½–2 hours. Remove the lid and continue simmering for a further 30 minutes to reduce. Skim off any fat, season, then strain and measure out 1.5 litres/2½ pints/6¼ cups.

2 Squeeze dry the soaked shiitake mushrooms, remove the stems and slice the caps into thin strips. Heat the oil in a large pan or wok and stir in the shallots, chillies and ginger. As the fragrance begins to rise, stir in the *nuoc mam*, followed by the stock.

3 Add the tofu, mushrooms and tomatoes and bring to the boil. Reduce the heat and simmer for 5–10 minutes. Season to taste and scatter the finely chopped fresh coriander over the top. Serve piping hot.

Serves four

115g/4oz/scant 2 cups dried shiitake mushrooms, soaked in water for 20 minutes

15ml/1 tbsp vegetable oil

2 shallots, halved and sliced

2 Thai chillies, seeded and sliced

4cm/1½in fresh root ginger, peeled and grated or finely chopped

15ml/1 tbsp *nuoc mam*

350g/12oz tofu, rinsed, drained and cut into bitesize cubes

4 tomatoes, skinned, seeded and cut into thin strips

salt and ground black pepper

1 bunch coriander (cilantro), stalks removed, finely chopped, to garnish

For the stock

1 meaty chicken carcass or 500g/1¼lb pork ribs

25g/1oz dried squid or shrimp, soaked in water for 15 minutes

2 onions, peeled and quartered

2 garlic cloves, crushed

7.5cm/3in fresh root ginger, chopped

15ml/1 tbsp *nuoc mam*

6 black peppercorns

2 star anise

4 cloves

1 cinnamon stick

sea salt

Energy 220Kcal/919kJ; Protein 12g; Carbohydrate 26g, of which sugars 4g; Fat 8g, of which saturates 1g; Cholesterol 0mg; Calcium 47.8mg; Fibre 1.1g; Sodium 500mg.

Winter melon soup with lily buds, coriander and mint

This soup uses two traditional South-east Asian ingredients – winter melon to absorb the flavours, and lily buds to lift the broth with a floral scent. When choosing lily buds, make sure they are light golden in colour.

1 To make the stock, drain and rinse the dried shrimp. Put the pork ribs in a large pan and cover with 2 litres/3½ pints/8 cups water. Bring the water to the boil, skim off any fat, and add the dried shrimp and the remaining stock ingredients. Cover and simmer for 1½ hours, then skim off any foam or fat. Continue simmering, uncovered, for a further 30 minutes. Strain and check the seasoning. You should have about 1.5 litres/2½ pints/6¼ cups.

2 Halve the winter melon lengthways and remove the seeds and inner membrane. Finely slice the flesh into half-moons. Squeeze the soaked lily buds dry and tie them in a knot.

3 Bring the stock to the boil in a deep pan or wok. Reduce the heat and add the winter melon and lily buds. Simmer for 15–20 minutes, or until the winter melon is tender. Season to taste, and scatter the herbs over the top.

Serves four

350g/12oz winter melon

25g/1oz light golden lily buds, soaked in hot water for 20 minutes

salt and ground black pepper

1 small bunch each coriander (cilantro) and mint, stalks removed, leaves chopped, to serve

For the stock

25g/1oz dried shrimp, soaked in water for 15 minutes

500g/1¼lb pork ribs

1 onion, peeled and quartered

175g/6oz carrots, peeled and cut into chunks

15ml/1 tbsp *nuoc mam*

15ml/1 tbsp soy sauce

4 black peppercorns

Energy 46Kcal/198kJ; Protein 2g; Carbohydrate 9g, of which sugars 4g; Fat 0g, of which saturates 0g; Cholesterol 0mg; Calcium 90mg; Fibre 1.4g; Sodium 400mg.

Broth with stuffed cabbage leaves

The origins of this soup, called *canh bap cuon*, could be attributed to the French dish *chou farci*, or to the ancient Chinese tradition of cooking dumplings in a clear broth. This Vietnamese soup is often reserved for special occasions such as the New Year, *Tet*.

1 To make the chicken stock, put the chicken carcass into a deep pan. Add all the other stock ingredients except the sea salt and pour over 2 litres/3½ pints/8 cups of water. Bring to the boil, and boil for a few minutes, skim off any foam, then reduce the heat and simmer gently with the lid on for 1½–2 hours.

2 Remove the lid and simmer for a further 30 minutes to reduce the stock. Skim off any fat, season with sea salt, then strain the stock and measure out 1.5 litres/2½ pints/6¼ cups. It is important to skim off any froth or fat, so that the broth is light and fragrant.

3 Blanch the cabbage leaves in boiling water for about 2 minutes, or until tender. Remove with a slotted spoon and refresh under cold water. Add the green tops of the spring onions to the boiling water and blanch for a minute, or until tender, then drain and refresh under cold water. Carefully tear each piece into five thin strips and set aside.

4 Squeeze dry the cloud ear mushrooms, then trim and finely chop and mix with the pork, prawns, spring onion whites, chilli, *nuoc mam* and soy sauce. Lay a cabbage leaf flat on a surface and place a teaspoon of the filling about 1cm/½in from the bottom edge – the edge nearest to you.

5 Fold this bottom edge over the filling, and then fold in the sides of the leaf to seal it. Roll all the way to the top of the leaf to form a tight bundle. Wrap a piece of blanched spring onion green around the bundle and tie it so that it holds together. Repeat with the remaining leaves and filling.

6 Bring the stock to the boil in a wok or deep pan. Stir in the finely sliced ginger, then reduce the heat and drop in the cabbage bundles. Bubble very gently over a low heat for about 20 minutes to ensure that the filling is thoroughly cooked. Serve immediately, ladled into bowls with a sprinkling of fresh coriander leaves.

Serves four

10 Chinese leaves (Chinese cabbage) or Savoy cabbage leaves, halved, main ribs removed

4 spring onions (scallions), green tops left whole, white part finely chopped

5–6 dried cloud ear (wood ear) mushrooms, soaked in hot water for 15 minutes

115g/4oz minced (ground) pork

115g/4oz prawns (shrimp), shelled, deveined and finely chopped

1 Thai chilli, seeded and chopped

30ml/2 tbsp *nuoc mam*

15ml/1 tbsp soy sauce

4cm/1½in fresh root ginger, peeled and very finely sliced

chopped fresh coriander (cilantro), to garnish

For the stock

1 meaty chicken carcass

2 onions, peeled and quartered

4 garlic cloves, crushed

4cm/1½in fresh root ginger, chopped

30ml/2 tbsp *nuoc mam*

30ml/2 tbsp soy sauce

6 black peppercorns

a few sprigs of fresh thyme

sea salt

Energy 106Kcal/447kJ; Protein 14g; Carbohydrate 9g, of which sugars 1g; Fat 2g, of which saturates 0g; Cholesterol 77mg; Calcium 43mg; Fibre 0.3g; Sodium 1100mg.

Duck and nut soup with Chinese red dates

This northern Vietnamese dish is satisfying and delicious. Packed with nuts and sweetened with dried Chinese red dates (also called jujubes), it resembles neither a soup nor a stew, but something in between. Served on its own, or with rice and pickles, it is a meal in itself.

1 Heat the oil in a wok or heavy pan. Brown the duck legs in the oil and drain on kitchen paper.

2 Bring 2 litres/3½ pints/7¾ cups water to the boil. Reduce the heat and add the coconut juice, *nuoc mam*, lemon grass and duck legs. Cover the pan and simmer over a gentle heat for 2–3 hours. Skim off any fat.

3 Add the nuts and dates and cook for 40 minutes, until the chestnuts are soft and the duck is very tender. Skim off any fat, season to taste and scatter the basil leaves over the top to serve.

Cook's Tip To extract the coconut juice, pierce the eyes on top of the coconut and then turn it upside down over a bowl.

Serves four

30–45ml/2–3 tbsp vegetable oil

4 duck legs, split into thighs and drumsticks

juice of 1 coconut

60ml/4 tbsp *nuoc mam*

4 lemon grass stalks, bruised

12 chestnuts, peeled

90g/3½oz unsalted cashew nuts, roasted

90g/3½oz unsalted almonds, roasted

90g/3½oz unsalted peanuts, roasted

12 Chinese red dates

sea salt and ground black pepper

1 bunch fresh basil leaves, to garnish

Variation If you cannot find Chinese red dates (jujubes), they can be replaced with ordinary dates.

Energy 604Kcal/2512kJ; Protein 44g; Carbohydrate 9g, of which sugars 3.6g; Fat 44g, of which saturates 9.2g; Cholesterol 165mg; Calcium 49mg; Fibre 3.1g; Sodium 230mg.

Serves four to six

450g/1lb fresh lotus root, peeled and thinly sliced

ground black pepper

1 red chilli, seeded and finely sliced, and 1 small bunch basil leaves, to garnish

For the stock

450g/1lb pork ribs

1 onion, quartered

2 carrots, cut into chunks

25g/1oz dried squid or dried shrimp, soaked in water for 30 minutes, rinsed and drained

15ml/1 tbsp *nuoc mam*

15ml/1 tbsp soy sauce

6 black peppercorns

sea salt

Pork and lotus root broth

This Vietnamese soup is from the central region of the country, where the lotus – a type of water lily – is used in many dishes. In this clear broth, which is served as an appetizer, the thin, round slices of fresh lotus root look like delicate flowers floating in water.

1 Put the ribs into a pan and cover with 1.5 litres/2½ pints/6¼ cups water. Bring to the boil, skim off any fat, and add the other ingredients. Reduce the heat, cover, and simmer for 2 hours.

2 Take off the lid and simmer for a further 30 minutes to reduce the stock. Strain the stock and shred the meat off the pork ribs.

3 Pour the stock back into the pan and bring it to the boil. Reduce the heat and add the lotus root. Partially cover the pan and simmer gently for 30–40 minutes, until the lotus root is tender.

4 Stir in the shredded meat and season the broth with salt and pepper. Ladle the soup into bowls and garnish with the chilli and basil leaves.

Energy 181Kcal/756kJ; Protein 23.8g; Carbohydrate 4g, of which sugars 3.1g; Fat 7.8g, of which saturates 2.7g; Cholesterol 74mg; Calcium 65mg; Fibre 1.4g; Sodium 270mg.

Saigon pork and prawn soup

Hu tieu do bien is a speciality of Ho Chi Minh City (formerly Saigon), where the pork stock is enhanced with the intense sweet and smoky flavour of dried squid. It is also a popular soup in Cambodia, where it is called *k'tiao*.

1 To make the stock, soak the dried squid in water for 30 minutes, rinse and drain. Put the ribs in a large pan and cover with approximately 2.5 litres/4½ pints/10 cups water. Bring to the boil, skim off any fat, and add the dried squid with the remaining stock ingredients. Cover the pan and simmer for 1 hour, then skim off any foam or fat and continue to simmer, uncovered, for a further 1½ hours.

2 Strain the stock and check the seasoning. You should have roughly 2 litres/3½ pints/ 8 cups. Pour the stock into a wok or deep pan and bring to the boil. Reduce the heat, add the pork tenderloin and simmer for 25 minutes. Lift the tenderloin out of the stock, place it on a board and cut it into thin slices. Meanwhile, keep the stock simmering gently over a low heat.

3 Bring a pan of water to the boil. Drain the rice sticks and add to the water. Cook for about 5 minutes, or until tender, separating them with chopsticks if they stick together. Drain the rice sticks and divide them among four warm bowls.

4 Drop the prawns into the simmering stock for 1 minute. Lift them out with a slotted spoon and layer them with the slices of pork on top of the rice sticks. Ladle the hot stock over them and sprinkle with beansprouts, spring onions, chillies, garlic and herbs. Serve with a wedge of lime to squeeze over and *nuoc cham* to splash on top.

Serves four

225g/8oz pork tenderloin

225g/8oz dried rice sticks (vermicelli), soaked in lukewarm water for 20 minutes

20 prawns (shrimp), shelled and deveined

115g/4oz/½ cup beansprouts

2 spring onions (scallions), finely sliced

2 green or red Thai chillies, seeded and finely sliced

1 garlic clove, finely sliced

1 bunch each coriander (cilantro) and basil, stalks removed, leaves roughly chopped

1 lime, cut into quarters, and *nuoc cham*, to serve

For the stock

25g/1oz dried squid

675g/1½lb pork ribs

1 onion, peeled and quartered

225g/8oz carrots, peeled and cut into chunks

15ml/1 tbsp *nuoc mam*

15ml/1 tbsp soy sauce

6 black peppercorns

salt

Cook's tip To serve the soup on its own, add bitesize pieces of soaked dried shiitake mushrooms or cubes of firm tofu.

Energy 319Kcal/1339kJ; Protein 22g; Carbohydrate 50g, of which sugars 1g; Fat 3g, of which saturates 0g; Cholesterol 49mg; Calcium 91mg; Fibre 0.6g; Sodium 500mg.

Sour broth with water spinach and beef

Serves four to six

30ml/2 tbsp *nuoc mam*

5ml/1 tsp sugar

175g/6oz beef fillet, finely sliced across the grain into 2.5cm/1in strips

1.2 litres/2 pints/5 cups beef or chicken stock

175g/6oz water spinach, trimmed, rinsed, leaves and stalks separated

juice of 1 lemon

ground black pepper

1 red or green chilli, seeded and finely sliced, to garnish

Water spinach is a popular vegetable in Vietnam. When cooked, the stems remain crunchy while the leaves soften, lending a delightful contrast of texture to the dish. Served as an appetizer, this is a light soup with tender bites of beef and sour notes of lemon juice.

1 In a bowl, stir the *nuoc mam* with the sugar until it has dissolved. Toss in the beef strips and leave to marinate for 30 minutes. Pour the stock into a pan and bring it to the boil. Reduce the heat and add the water spinach. Stir in the lemon juice and season with pepper.

2 Place the meat strips in individual bowls and ladle the hot broth over the top. Garnish with chillies and serve.

Variation You can sprinkle coriander and mint or fried garlic and ginger over this soup.

Energy 61Kcal/254kJ; Protein 7.4g; Carbohydrate 1.2g, of which sugars 1.1g; Fat 3g, of which saturates 1.1g; Cholesterol 17mg; Calcium 51mg; Fibre 0.6g; Sodium 600mg.

Beef noodle soup

Some would say that this classic noodle soup – known as *pho* – is Vietnam in a bowl. Made with beef (*pho bo*) or chicken (*pho ga*), it is Vietnamese fast food, street food, working men's food and family food. It is nutritious and filling, and makes an intensely satisfying meal.

1 To make the stock, put the oxtail into a large, deep pan and cover it with water. Bring it to the boil and blanch the meat for about 10 minutes. Drain the meat, rinsing off any scum, and clean out the pan. Put the blanched oxtail back into the pan with the other stock ingredients, apart from the *nuoc mam* and salt, and cover with about 3 litres/5¼ pints/12 cups water. Bring it to the boil, reduce the heat and simmer, covered, for 2–3 hours.

2 Remove the lid and simmer for another hour, until the stock has reduced to about 2 litres/3½ pints/8 cups. Skim off any fat, then strain the stock into another pan.

3 Cut the beef sirloin across the grain into thin pieces the size of the heel of your hand. Bring the stock to the boil once more, stir in the *nuoc mam*, season to taste, then reduce the heat and leave the stock simmering until ready to use.

4 Meanwhile, bring a pan filled with water to the boil, drain the rice sticks and add to the water. Cook for about 5 minutes or until tender – you may need to separate them with a pair of chopsticks if they look as though they are sticking together.

5 Drain the noodles and divide them equally among six wide soup bowls. Top each serving with the slices of beef, onion, spring onions, chillies and beansprouts.

6 Ladle the hot stock over the top of these ingredients, top with the fresh herbs and serve with the lime wedges to squeeze over. Pass around the hoisin sauce, *nuoc mam* or *nuoc cham* for those who like a little sweetening, fish flavouring or extra fire.

Cook's tips The key to *pho* is a tasty, light stock flavoured with ginger, cinnamon, cloves and star anise, so it is worth cooking it slowly and leaving it to stand overnight to allow the flavours to develop fully. To enjoy this dish, use chopsticks to lift the noodles through the layers of flavouring and slurp them up. This is the essence of Vietnam.

Serves six

250g/9oz beef sirloin

500g/1¼lb dried noodles, soaked in lukewarm water for 20 minutes

1 onion, halved and finely sliced

6–8 spring onions (scallions), cut into long pieces

2–3 red Thai chillies, seeded and finely sliced

115g/4oz/½ cup beansprouts

1 large bunch each fresh coriander (cilantro) and mint, stalks removed, leaves chopped

2 limes, cut in wedges, and hoisin sauce, *nuoc mam* or *nuoc cham*, to serve

For the stock

1.5kg/3lb 5oz oxtail, trimmed of fat and cut into thick pieces

1kg/2¼lb beef shank or brisket

2 large onions, peeled and quartered

2 carrots, peeled and cut into chunks

7.5cm/3in fresh root ginger, cut into chunks

6 cloves

2 cinnamon sticks

6 star anise

5ml/1 tsp black peppercorns

30ml/2 tbsp soy sauce

45–60ml/3–4 tbsp *nuoc mam*

salt

Energy 391Kcal/1635kJ; Protein 16g; Carbohydrate 74g, of which sugars 3g; Fat 2g, of which saturates 1g; Cholesterol 21mg; Calcium 62mg; Fibre 0.8g; Sodium 600mg.

Hot-and-sour fish soup

This tangy soup, *canh chua ca*, is found throughout South-east Asia – with the balance of hot, sweet and sour flavours varying from Cambodia to Vietnam. Chillies provide the heat, tamarind produces the tartness, and the delicious sweetness comes from pineapple.

1 Cut the fish into bitesize pieces, mix with the *nuoc mam* and garlic and leave to marinate. Save the head, tail and bones for the stock. Drain and rinse the soaked, dried squid.

2 Heat the oil in a deep pan and stir in the spring onions, shallots, ginger, lemon grass and dried squid. Add the reserved fish head, tail and bones, and sauté them gently for a minute or two. Pour in 1.2 litres/2 pints/5 cups water and bring to the boil. Reduce the heat and simmer for 30 minutes.

3 Strain the stock into another deep pan and bring to the boil. Stir in the tamarind paste, chillies, sugar and *nuoc mam* and simmer for 2–3 minutes. Add the pineapple, tomatoes and bamboo shoots and simmer for a further 2–3 minutes. Stir in the fish pieces and the chopped fresh coriander, and cook until the fish turns opaque.

4 Season to taste and ladle the soup into hot bowls. Garnish with beansprouts and dill, and serve with the lime quarters to squeeze over.

Serves four

1 catfish, sea bass or red snapper, about 1kg/2¼lb, filleted

30ml/2 tbsp *nuoc mam*

2 garlic cloves, finely chopped

25g/1oz dried squid, soaked in water for 30 minutes

15ml/1 tbsp vegetable oil

2 spring onions (scallions), sliced

2 shallots, sliced

4cm/1½in fresh root ginger, peeled and chopped

2–3 lemon grass stalks, cut into strips and crushed

30ml/2 tbsp tamarind paste

2–3 Thai chillies, seeded and sliced

15ml/1 tbsp sugar

30–45ml/2–3 tbsp *nuoc mam*

225g/8oz fresh pineapple, peeled and diced

3 tomatoes, skinned, seeded and roughly chopped

50g/2oz canned sliced bamboo shoots, drained

1 small bunch fresh coriander (cilantro), stalks removed, leaves finely chopped

salt and ground black pepper

115g/4oz/½cup beansprouts and 1 bunch dill, fronds roughly chopped, to garnish

1 lime, cut into quarters, to serve

Energy 335Kcal/1415kJ; Protein 44g; Carbohydrate 24g, of which sugars 19g; Fat 7g, of which saturates 1g; Cholesterol 108mg; Calcium 138mg; Fibre 2.3g; Sodium 1.2g.

Serves four

15ml/1 tbsp vegetable oil

2 shallots, finely chopped

2 garlic cloves, finely chopped

15ml/1 tbsp rice flour or cornflour (cornstarch)

225g/8oz/1⅓ cups cooked crab meat, chopped into small pieces

450g/1lb preserved asparagus, finely chopped, or 450g/1lb fresh asparagus, trimmed and steamed

salt and ground black pepper

basil and coriander (cilantro) leaves, to garnish

nuoc cham, to serve

For the stock

1 meaty chicken carcass

25g/1oz dried shrimp, soaked in water for 30 minutes, rinsed and drained

2 onions, peeled and quartered

2 garlic cloves, crushed

15ml/1 tbsp *nuoc mam*

6 black peppercorns

sea salt

Cook's tip In households close to the sea, where large crabs can be found in abundance, this soup may be made using a generous quantity of fresh crab. You can increase the quantity of crab meat as much as you like, to make a soup that is very rich and filling.

Crab and asparagus soup with *nuoc cham*

In this delicious soup the recipe has clearly been adapted from the classic French asparagus *velouté* to produce a much meatier version that has more texture, with the Vietnamese stamp of *nuoc cham* and *nuoc mam*.

1 To make the stock, put the chicken carcass into a large pan. Add all the other stock ingredients, except the salt, and pour in 2 litres/3½ pints/8 cups water. Bring to the boil, cook for a few minutes, skim off any foam, then reduce the heat and simmer with the lid on for 1½–2 hours. Remove the lid and simmer for a further 30 minutes to reduce the stock. Skim off any fat, season, then strain the stock and measure out 1.5 litres/2½ pints/6¼ cups.

2 Heat the oil in a deep pan or wok. Stir in the shallots and garlic, until they begin to colour. Remove from the heat, stir in the flour, and then pour in the stock. Put the pan back over the heat and bring to the boil, stirring constantly, until smooth.

3 Add the crab meat and asparagus, reduce the heat and leave to simmer for 15–20 minutes. Season to taste with salt and pepper, then ladle the soup into bowls, garnish with fresh basil and coriander leaves, and serve with a splash of *nuoc cham*.

Energy 143Kcal/593kJ; Protein 45g; Carbohydrate 4g, of which sugars 2g; Fat 7g, of which saturates 1g; Cholesterol 41mg; Calcium 29mg; Fibre 3.5g; Sodium 800mg.

CAMBODIA

Though largely Chinese in essence, Cambodian or Khmer cuisine strongly reflects tones of Indian, Laotian, Thai and French cooking. The tropical and sub-tropical climate yields herbs and spices common to the entire South-east Asian region, and dishes are enticingly perfumed with lime, lemon grass and other exotic herbs. There is also rich sustenance with beef, pork and seafood added. The French influence has not been lost, as it is traditional to serve soups with crusty baguettes, especially in the south.

Chicken rice soup with lemon grass

Shnor chrook is Cambodia's answer to the classic chicken noodle soup that is popular in the West. Light and refreshing, it is the perfect choice for a hot day, as well as a great pick-me-up when you are feeling low or tired.

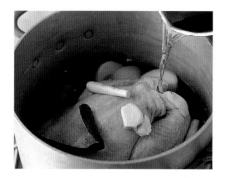 

1 Put the chicken into a deep pan. Add all the other stock ingredients and pour in 2 litres/3½ pints/7¾ cups water. Bring to the boil for a few minutes, then reduce the heat and simmer gently with the lid on for 2 hours.

2 Skim off any fat from the stock, strain and reserve. Remove the skin from the chicken and shred the meat. Set aside.

3 Pour the stock back into the deep pan and bring to the boil. Reduce the heat and stir in the lemon grass stalks and fish sauce. Stir in the rice and simmer, uncovered, for about 40 minutes. Add the shredded chicken and season to taste.

4 Ladle the piping hot soup into warmed individual bowls, garnish with chopped coriander and the thin strips of chilli, and serve with lime wedges to squeeze over.

Cook's tip The fresh, citrus aroma of lemon grass and lime, combined with the warmth of the chillies, is invigorating and awakens the senses. However, many Cambodians and Vietnamese often spike the soup with additional chillies as a garnish, or served on the side. Variations of this soup crop up all over Cambodia and Vietnam, where it is often served as a meal in itself.

Serves four

2 lemon grass stalks, trimmed, cut into 3 pieces, and lightly bruised

15ml/1 tbsp fish sauce, such as *nam pla*

90g/3½oz/½ cup short grain rice, rinsed

1 small bunch coriander (cilantro) leaves, finely chopped, and 1 green or red chilli, seeded and cut into thin strips, to garnish

1 lime, cut in wedges, to serve

sea salt

ground black pepper

For the stock

1 small chicken or 2 meaty chicken legs

1 onion, quartered

2 cloves garlic, crushed

25g/1oz fresh root ginger, sliced

2 lemon grass stalks, cut in half lengthwise and bruised

2 dried red chillies

30ml/2 tbsp *nuoc mam*

Energy 147Kcal/615kJ; Protein 12.8g; Carbohydrate 19.8g, of which sugars 1.4g; Fat 1.7g, of which saturates 0.4g; Cholesterol 53mg; Calcium 37mg; Fibre 0.8g; Sodium 320mg.

Duck and preserved lime soup

This rich Cambodian soup, *samlaw tiah*, originates in the Chiu Chow region of southern China. This recipe can be made with chicken stock and leftover duck meat from a roasted duck, or by roasting a duck and then slicing off the breast and thigh meat for the soup.

1 Place the duck in a large pan with enough water to cover. Season with salt and pepper and bring the water to the boil. Reduce the heat, cover the pot, and simmer for 1½ hours.

2 Add the preserved limes and ginger. Continue to simmer for another hour, skimming off the fat from time to time, until the liquid has reduced a little and the duck is so tender that it almost falls off the bone.

3 Meanwhile, heat some vegetable oil in a wok. Stir in the ginger and garlic strips and fry until gold and crispy. Drain well on kitchen paper and set aside for garnishing.

4 Remove the duck from the broth and shred the meat into individual bowls. Check the broth for seasoning, then ladle it over the duck in the bowls. Scatter the spring onions with the fried ginger and garlic over the top and serve.

Serves four to six

1 lean duck, approximately 1.5kg/3lb 5oz

2 preserved limes

25g/1oz fresh root ginger, thinly sliced

sea salt and ground black pepper

For the garnish

vegetable oil, for frying

25g/1oz fresh root ginger, thinly sliced into strips

2 garlic cloves, thinly sliced into strips

2 spring onions (scallions), finely sliced

Cook's tip With the addition of noodles, this soup could be substantial enough to be served as a meal in itself.

Energy 124Kcal/520kJ; Protein 19.8g; Carbohydrate 0.3g, of which sugars 0.3g; Fat 6.5g, of which saturates 1.3g; Cholesterol 110mg; Calcium 19mg; Fibre 0g; Sodium 100mg.

Serves four

75g/3oz/scant ½ cup long grain rice, well rinsed

250ml/8fl oz/1 cup coconut milk

30ml/2 tbsp *tuk prahoc*

2 lemon grass stalks, trimmed and crushed

25g/1oz galangal, thinly sliced

2–3 Thai chillies

4 garlic cloves, crushed

15ml/1 tbsp palm sugar

1 fresh bamboo shoot, peeled, boiled in water for 10 minutes, and sliced

450g/1lb freshwater fish fillets, such as carp or catfish, skinned and cut into bitesize pieces

1 small bunch fresh basil leaves

1 small bunch fresh coriander (cilantro), chopped, and 1 chilli, finely sliced, to garnish

rice or noodles, to serve

For the stock

675g/1½lb pork ribs

1 onion, quartered

225g/8oz carrots, cut into chunks

25g/1oz dried squid or dried shrimp, soaked in water for 30 minutes, rinsed and drained

15ml/1 tbsp *nuoc mam*

15ml/1 tbsp soy sauce

6 black peppercorns

salt

Bamboo, fish and rice soup

This is a refreshing Khmer soup made with freshwater fish. A speciality of Phnom Penh, *samlaw trapeang* is flavoured with coconut milk, the fermented fish extract *tuk prahoc*, lemon grass and galangal – some of Cambodia's principal ingredients.

1 To prepare the stock, put the ribs in a large pan and cover with 2.5 litres/4¼ pints/ 10 cups water. Bring to the boil, skim off any fat, and add the remaining stock ingredients. Cover the pan and simmer for 1 hour, then skim off any foam or fat.

2 Simmer the stock, uncovered, for a further 1–1½ hours, until it has reduced. Check the seasoning and strain the stock into another pan. There should be approximately 2 litres/3½ pints/7¾ cups of stock.

3 Bring the pan of stock to the boil. Stir in the rice and reduce the heat. Add the coconut milk, *tuk prahoc*, lemon grass, galangal, chillies, garlic and sugar. Simmer for about 10 minutes to let the flavours mingle. The rice should be just cooked, with bite to it.

4 Add the sliced bamboo shoot and the pieces of fish. Simmer for 5 minutes, until the fish is cooked. Check the seasoning and stir in the basil leaves. Ladle the soup into bowls, garnish with the chopped coriander and chilli, and serve with the rice or noodles.

Energy 181Kcal/763kJ; Protein 22.8g; Carbohydrate 19.6g, of which sugars 4.3g; Fat 1.3g, of which saturates 0.2g; Cholesterol 52mg; Calcium 64mg; Fibre 0.9g; Sodium 150mg.

Spicy beef and aubergine soup

A wonderful Khmer dish, this soup – *samlaw machou kroeung* – is sweet, spicy and tangy. The flavour is mainly derived from the Cambodian herbal condiment *kroeung*, and the fermented fish extract *tuk trey*.

1 To make the stock, put the beef shanks into a deep pan with all the other stock ingredients, apart from the soy sauce and *tuk trey*. Cover with 3 litres/5 pints/12 cups water and bring it to the boil. Reduce the heat and simmer, covered, for 2–3 hours.

2 Soak the New Mexico chillies in water for 30 minutes. Split them open, remove the seeds and scrape out the pulp with a spoon.

3 Take the lid off the stock and stir in the remaining two ingredients. Simmer, uncovered, for another hour, until the stock has reduced to about 2 litres/3½ pints/7¾ cups. Skim off any fat, strain the stock into a bowl and put aside. Lift the meat on to a plate, tear it into thin strips and put half of it aside for the soup.

4 Heat the oil in a wok or heavy pan. Stir in the *kroeung* along with the pulp from the New Mexico chillies and the whole Thai chillies. Stir the spicy paste as it sizzles, until it begins to darken. Add the tamarind extract, *tuk trey*, sugar and the reserved stock. Stir well and bring to the boil.

5 Reduce the heat and add the reserved beef, aubergines and watercress or rocket. Continue cooking for about 20 minutes to allow the flavours to mingle.

6 Meanwhile, dry-fry the curry leaves. Heat a small, heavy pan over a high heat, add the curry leaves and cook them until they begin to crackle. Transfer them to a plate and set aside.

7 Season the soup to taste. Stir in half the curry leaves and ladle the soup into individual bowls. Scatter the remaining curry leaves over the top and serve.

Cook's tip For a greater depth of flavour, you can dry-roast the New Mexico chillies before soaking them in water.

Serves six

4 dried New Mexico chillies

15ml/1 tbsp vegetable oil

75ml/5 tbsp *kroeung*

2–3 fresh or dried red Thai chillies

75ml/5 tbsp tamarind extract

15–30ml/1–2 tbsp *tuk trey*

30ml/2 tbsp palm sugar

12 Thai aubergines (eggplants), with stems removed and cut into bitesize chunks

1 bunch watercress or rocket (arugula), trimmed and chopped

1 handful fresh curry leaves

sea salt and ground black pepper

For the stock

1kg/2¼lb beef shanks or brisket

2 large onions, quartered

2–3 carrots, cut into chunks

90g/3½oz fresh root ginger, sliced

2 cinnamon sticks

4 star anise

5ml/1 tsp black peppercorns

30ml/2 tbsp soy sauce

45–60ml/3–4 tbsp *tuk trey*

Energy 303Kcal/1276kJ; Protein 37g; Carbohydrate 16.5g, of which sugars 14.5g; Fat 10.6g, of which saturates 4.2g; Cholesterol 90mg; Calcium 35mg; Fibre 2.4g; Sodium 300mg.

Index

bacon
  Hokkien Prawn Noodle
    Soup 51
Bamboo, Fish and Rice Soup 93
beef
  Beef and Heart of Palm
    Soup 72
  Beef Noodle Soup 84–5
  Sour Broth with Water Spinach
    and Beef 83
  Spicy Aubergine Soup with
    Beef and Lime 62–3
  Spicy Beef and Aubergine
    Soup 94–5
  Spicy Tripe Soup with Lemon
    Grass and Lime 64–5
Broth with Stuffed Cabbage
  Leaves 78–9

Cellophane Noodle Soup 29
Chiang Mai Noodle Soup 32
chicken
  Broth with Stuffed Cabbage
    Leaves 78–9
  Chiang Mai Noodle Soup 32
  Chicken and Ginger Broth with
    Papaya 69
  Chicken Rice Soup with
    Lemon Grass 90–1
  Chicken Soup with Coconut 68
  Crab and Asparagus Soup with
    Nuoc Cham 87
  Eurasian Curried Soup 49
  Galangal, Chicken and Coconut
    Soup 30–1
  Hokkien Prawn Noodle
    Soup 51
  Indonesian Chicken Broth 60–1
  Spicy Chicken Soup 48
  Tofu Soup with Mushrooms,
    Tomato, Ginger and
    Coriander 76
cockles
  Singapore Laksa 52–3
Coconut and Seafood Soup 37
Colonial Rice Soup with Pork and
  Roasted Garlic 71
Crab and Asparagus Soup with
  Nuoc Cham 87

duck
  Duck and Nut Soup with
    Chinese Red Dates 80
  Duck and Preserved Lime
    Soup 92

Eurasian Curried Soup 49

fish
  Bamboo, Fish and Rice Soup 93
  Fish Ball Soup 41
  Hot and Sour Filipino Fish
    Soup 73
  Hot-and-sour Fish Soup 86
  Malaysian Hot and Sour Fish
    Soup 40
  Smoked Mackerel and
    Tomato Soup 34

Galangal, Chicken and Coconut
  Soup 30–1

Hokkien Prawn Noodle Soup 51
Hot and Sour Filipino Fish
  Soup 73
Hot-and-sour Fish Soup 86
Hot-and-sour Prawn Soup 30–1
Hot and Sweet Vegetable and
  Tofu Soup 26

Indonesian Chicken Broth 60–1

Malaysian Hot and Sour Fish
  Soup 40
Mixed Vegetable Soup 27
Mooli and Prawn Soup 43

noodles
  Beef Noodle Soup 84–5
  Cellophane Noodle Soup 29
  Chiang Mai Noodle Soup 32
  Fish Ball Soup 41
  Hokkien Prawn Noodle
    Soup 51
  Noodles in Spicy Tangy
    Soup 44–5
  Singapore Laksa 52–3
  Spicy Chicken Soup 48
Northern Prawn and Squash
  Soup 36

Omelette Soup 28

papaya
  Chicken and Ginger Broth
    with Papaya 69
  Unripe Papaya Soup 56–7
pork
  Bamboo, Fish and Rice Soup 93
  Broth with Stuffed Cabbage
    Leaves 78–9

Colonial Rice Soup with Pork
  and Roasted Garlic 71
Hokkien Prawn Noodle
  Soup 51
Pork Bone Tea 50
Pork and Lotus Root Broth 81
Rice Porridge 33
Saigon Pork and Prawn
  Soup 82
Tamarind Pork and Vegetable
  Soup 70
Won Ton Soup 42
prawns (shrimp)
  Broth with Stuffed Cabbage
    Leaves 78–9
  Coconut and Seafood Soup 37
  Hokkien Prawn Noodle Soup 51
  Hot and Sour Filipino
    Fish Soup 73
  Hot-and-sour Prawn
    Soup 30–1
  Mooli and Prawn Soup 43
  Noodles in Spicy Tangy
    Soup 44–5
  Northern Prawn and Squash
    Soup 36
  Pumpkin, Prawn and Coconut
    Soup 35
  Saigon Pork and Prawn Soup 82
  Singapore Laksa 52–3
  Won Ton Soup 42
Pumpkin, Prawn and Coconut
  Soup 35
Pumpkin, Snake Bean and
  Bamboo Soup with
  Coconut 58–9

Rice Porridge 33

Saigon Pork and Prawn Soup 82
shrimp, dried
  Bamboo, Fish and Rice Soup 93
  Crab and Asparagus Soup with
    Nuoc Cham 87
  Hokkien Prawn Noodle Soup 51
  Noodles in Spicy Tangy
    Soup 44–5
  Pork and Lotus Root Broth 81
  Pumpkin, Prawn and Coconut
    Soup 35
  Singapore Laksa 52–3
  Tofu Soup with Mushrooms,
    Tomato, Ginger and
    Coriander 76
  Winter Melon Soup with Lily
    Buds, Coriander and Mint 77
Singapore Laksa 52–3
Smoked Mackerel and Tomato
  Soup 34
Sour Broth with Water Spinach
  and Beef 83

Spicy Aubergine Soup with Beef
  and Lime 62–3
Spicy Beef and Aubergine Soup
  94–5
Spicy Chicken Soup 48
Spicy Tripe Soup with Lemon
  Grass and Lime 64–5
squid
  Bamboo, Fish and Rice
    Soup 93
  Coconut and Seafood Soup 37
  Hot-and-sour Fish Soup 86
  Pork and Lotus Root Broth 81
  Saigon Pork and Prawn
    Soup 82
  Singapore Laksa 52–3
  Tofu Soup with Mushrooms,
    Tomato, Ginger and
    Coriander 76

Tamarind Pork and Vegetable
  Soup 70
tofu
  Hot and Sweet Vegetable and
    Tofu Soup 26
  Mixed Vegetable Soup 27
  Noodles in Spicy Tangy
    Soup 44–5
  Tofu Soup with Mushrooms,
    Tomato, Ginger and
    Coriander 76

Unripe Papaya Soup 56–7

vegetables
  Cellophane Noodle Soup 29
  Hot and Sweet Vegetable and
    Tofu Soup 26
  Mixed Vegetable Soup 27
  Northern Prawn and Squash
    Soup 36
  Omelette Soup 28
  Pumpkin, Snake Bean and
    Bamboo Soup with
    Coconut 58–9

Winter Melon Soup with Lily
  Buds, Coriander and Mint 77
Won Ton Soup 42